Battlefield Walks
DEVON

Battlefield Walks
DEVON

Rupert Matthews

F

FRANCES LINCOLN LIMITED
PUBLISHERS

Frances Lincoln Ltd
4 Torriano Mews
Torriano Avenue
London NW5 2RZ
www.franceslincoln.com

CONTENTS

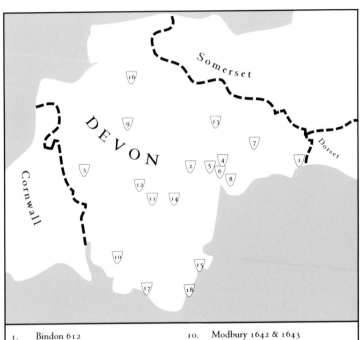

1.	Bindon 612	10.	Modbury 1642 & 1643
2.	Posbury 661	11.	Chagford 1643
3.	Lydford 997	12.	Sourton Down 1643
4.	Pinhoe 1001	13.	Tiverton 1645
5.	Exeter Castle 1136	14.	Bovey Heath 1646
6.	Exeter City 1497	15.	Dartmouth 1646
7.	Fenny Bridges 1549	16.	Torrington 1646
8.	Clyst St Mary 1549	17.	Salcombe Castle 1646
9.	Sampford Courtenay 1549	18.	Slapton Sands 1944

INTRODUCTION

Today Devon is a peaceful rural county famed for its English Riviera and other tourist attractions. It was not always so. Devon has seen more than its fair share of battles, sieges and campaigns. Few of these have involved foreign invaders, though some have, the periods of civil war giving rise to more bloodshed in Devon than any other cause. The county was heavily involved in the English Civil Wars of the seventeenth century as Cavalier and Roundhead clashed in Devon. Other conflicts were also played out here, including the Prayer Book Rebellion of the Reformation.

This book takes the reader on a journey through the military history of the county. It looks at eighteen of the more important battles and sieges that were fought here, putting them in their historic context and explaining how and why the battles were fought. The book looks at the developing weaponry and tactical face of warfare and how this affected the decisions of the commanders and the outcome of the struggles.

Each battle is described in the course of a walk around the battlefield. Generally, though not always, the walk follows the route followed by one commander or unit during the battle. The text describes the route to be taken, and where to pause to inspect the points where actions took place and events happened. All the routes have been walked by the author.

Sadly, not all the battlefields of Devon can be traced out on the ground. During the English Civil War, the Roundheads seized Plymouth, whereupon the Cavaliers put it under siege in 1643. The town held out for months before it was relieved. The events, personalities and places involved are well known. However, none of the Civil War defences remain, the entire area having been built over in Victorian times, and then pummelled by Hitler's Luftwaffe in the Second World War. A very different problem affects the great battle of 682 when the English crushed the British kingdom of Dumnonia: nobody knows where it was fought. We know it was somewhere east of the River Exe, but that is all.

Even when the site of a battle is known for certain problems still remain. The men fighting the battles had more important things to do than take careful notes about times and locations of individual events. All too often historical records are rather vague as to exactly where or when something happened. In writing this book I have tried hard to locate events on the ground as best I can. In the text I point out when a fact is known for certain, when it is probable and when it is merely conjectural. The maps of the battles should be viewed with this in mind.

This book has been a joy to research and to write. I must thank the good people of Devon for the warm welcomes that they extended to me during my visits to the places mentioned, and to research facilities in the counties. I would also like to thank Peter Kensell who helped out with some of the research. Finally, I must mention my wife for her patience during my absences.

I. BINDON
612

Distance:	4¼ miles.
Terrain:	Mostly over surfaced lanes which climb and descend steep slopes.
Public transport:	First Bus route x54 runs to Axmouth from Exeter.
Parking:	On-street parking in Axmouth, where the walk starts and finishes.
Refreshments:	Two pubs which serve meals and bar snacks.

The Dark Ages did not get their name for nothing. After the Romans left, the skills of writing and reading were restricted to very few people, and most of the books that did remain were subsequently lost, destroyed or simply fell to pieces. Not until the coming of literate Christians from Rome in the 590s does some semblance of recorded history return to Britain. During those lost years much happened: Roman Britain collapsed, King Arthur ruled, the English invaded and countless battles and campaigns were fought.

One of the very first military campaigns to be recorded as writing spread across Britain with Christianity was the Battle of Bindon Hill, fought in 612. In fact, the records of the event were not written down until some years later – perhaps as many as fifty or more – so the details are lacking, but the general outline of what happened has been preserved and it is possible to put together a good idea of the battle.

In 612 Britain was a very different place from how it appears today. The English then occupied only part of what is now England. In the north they were restricted to east of the Pennines, while in the south they had crossed neither the Severn nor the Axe. Nor were they united: Kent, Sussex, Wessex, East Anglia, Mercia

The estuary of the Ax at Axmouth. The Dumnonian army crossed the river somewhere near here on their way to invade Wessex.

and Northumbria were all independent kingdoms. The Welsh were no less disunited, with at least seven kingdoms in what is now Wales, plus Rheged in Cumbria and Strathclyde in southern Scotland. The counties now known as Cornwall and Devon, plus parts of Somerset, then formed the kingdom of Dumnonia.

It was the Welsh kingdom of Dumnonia and the English kingdom of Wessex that clashed at Bindon Hill.

At this date Wessex stretched from the Axe to Portsmouth and north to the Thames. It was one of the larger English kingdoms, though was rather smaller than Mercia or distant Northumbria. It was ruled by a king named Cynegils, who was probably half Welsh himself and may have been descended from the Celtic aristocracy of Hampshire as much as from English invaders.

This Cynegils was a pagan king of an English kingdom that relied almost exclusively on agriculture for its wealth. The complex trade routes of Roman Britain had vanished. There seems to have been only local trade in agricultural products such as flour or cheese. The ruler gained his wealth by taxing the farmers of his kingdom. For Cynegils and others like him, the only way to get richer was to be king of more land. It was this land hunger that drove the wars of the period.

Cynegils' father, King Ceolwulf, had occupied what is now Dorset in around the 590s. Whether this expansion of Wessex was by conquest, diplomacy or dynastic marriage we do not know, but it did bring Wessex on to the borders of Dumnonia.

This prosperous Welsh kingdom had emerged around the year 450 when the tribal aristocracy of the Dumnoni declared themselves independent of the authorities of post-Roman Britain. The records of Dumnonia have been lost, but later legend makes them among the most loyal supporters of King Arthur in his attempts to unite the post-Roman Britons against the invading English. They are also known to have acquired, apparently by marriage, a ruler from the royal dynasty of the Cornovii, a tribe in east-central Wales. In 612 Dumnonia covered all of Cornwall and Devon, and eastern Somerset at least as far north as Glastonbury.

We do not know the name of the King of Dumnonia in 612, but he was clearly in communication with the King of Gwent in south Wales. The rulers of Dumnonia and Gwent had both been eyeing the expanding might of Wessex with concern. When Ceolwulf died in 611 they decided that the time had come to strike. The new king, Cynegils, was young and inexperienced. His nobles may not have fully trusted the abilities of their new king. Wessex was vulnerable.

It seems that the King of Dumnonia believed that the people of Dorset, being mostly Celtic, were unhappy with rule by the English of Wessex. Perhaps the Dumnonians believed that they could raise a popular rebellion. They certainly launched the campaign by gathering a mighty army at Exeter, then marched east towards

Dorchester. Meanwhile, the King of Gwent had mustered his own army and was marching south-east past Gloucester toward Bath.

Cynegils decided to meet the Dumnonian threat first; perhaps that army was marching first. His scouts told him the route being taken by the invading Welsh, and he decided to meet them at Bindon Hill.

THE WALK

1. In Axmouth find the parish church at the western end of the village, just off the B3172.

In 612 this area was in a state of religious flux. The Christianity of post-Roman Britain was crumbling in the face of militant English paganism. There was probably no church here on the day of battle, but there may have been a wooden preaching cross. The village was certainly present in the form of a cluster of wooden buildings.

More significant from a military point of view was the old pre-Roman fort up on Hawkesdown Hill immediately north of the village. This mighty earthwork, now hidden in the hilltop trees and inaccessible to the public, had been built to command the estuary of the Axe. Although excavation by modern archaeologists here has been minimal, it does not seem to have been re-occupied and refortified in post-Roman times. In 612 it would have been available as a makeshift military post, but was no fortress. The kings of Wessex may have had a small lookout post permanently established there, but in any case Cynegils almost certainly had a scout or two up on the hill to look for the expected invasion.

That invasion came in the form of a powerful army led by the King of Dumnonia himself. A royal army such as this coming from

The view from the top of Bindon Hill down into the valley where the fighting took place.

a Welsh kingdom in the early seventh century would have based its weapons and tactics on late-Roman models, adapting them for the new conditions of recruitment and training which the Dumnonians faced.

The army would have been about 5,000 strong. The vast majority of these men would have been infantry. They were most likely equipped with large, round wooden shields about three feet in diameter and many had helmets. All were armed with a heavy thrusting spear about eight feet long, though the secondary side arm might have been a sword, axe or heavy knife. Some men had body armour, either of mail or of toughened leather.

There would also have been a few cavalrymen, perhaps around 300 or so. These men were more heavily armoured, wearing chain-mail shirts that reached to elbow and knee, as well as metal helmets and oval shields. Each mounted man carried a handful of throwing javelins, with a long, heavy sword at his belt and probably a knife as well. These men did not have stirrups to help them ride, but

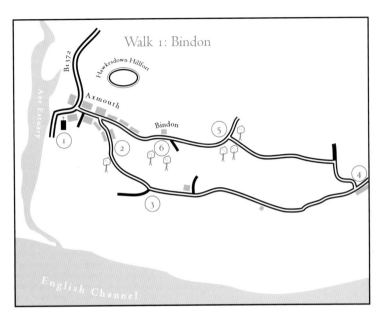

probably still retained the late-Roman saddle with its projecting horns that could be gripped by the knees.

Ideally the tactics used by such an army would have seen the infantry forming up in hollow squares or circles with the men three or four ranks deep. These defensive units remained fairly static on the battlefield, blocking fords or occupying high ground as the situation demanded. The cavalry moved swiftly around the battlefield, showering the enemy with javelins before wheeling away to safety. The feigned flight of the cavalry may have lured a disorganised enemy into charging the infantry blocs. If the opportunity offered itself the cavalry were capable of forming up knee to knee to deliver a formation-smashing charge with the riders wielding their long swords to murderous effect.

When used properly, such tactics could be awesomely effective.

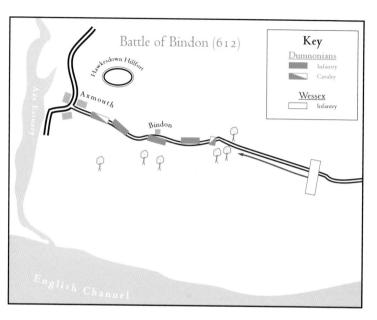

But by the early seventh century the kings of Dumnonia and other Welsh kingdoms were faced by a lack of riding horses for their cavalry and by the fact that their infantry were only partly trained farmers who lacked the iron discipline of the full-time Roman soldiers for whom such tactics had been devised.

Nevertheless, the King of Dumnonia must have been confident of success as he crossed the Axe and arrived in Axmouth. If there were English scouts up on Hawkesdown Hill, they either fled or were chased off. The Dumnonians formed up and marched east through Axmouth to pass up the narrow valley beyond and on to Dorchester.

2. From the church walk east along the B3172, then turn right into Chapel Street. Turn right again into Stepps Lane and

▷ The walk turns left here to descend into the valley in the footsteps of the Wessex army.

▽ The entrance to Bindon Manor marks the approximate area of the fiercest fighting.

climb steeply out of the valley to emerge on to the top of Bindon Hill.

3. Near the hillcrest, Stepps Lane bears left as a gravel track comes in from the right. Follow the lane east along the hilltop for about a mile.

4. At a cluster of buildings, turn left into Leggett Lane, signposted to Axmouth. Follow this lane for 200 yards. Where the lane turns sharp left and a track goes straight on, follow the lane left into Combe Road.

5. Continue west down Combe Road down the hill. Just beyond a patch of woodland the lane meets another. Turn left and continue along the valley.

It was here that Cynegils had probably been waiting. The valley narrows into a steep combe as it climbs up on to the high ground of the limestone hills that dominate the scenery. It seems that the English army was waiting here, ready to storm down the hill and attack the Welsh as they were strung out on the march. At this date Wessex could probably muster a force of 8,000 men in total. However, Cynegils needed to post some men to watch the advancing men of Gwent and more to watch his English neighbours of Mercia and Sussex. Perhaps he had some 4,000 men with him at Bindon.

At this date the English fought exclusively on foot, though some men had horses on which they could ride to battle or canter off to scout or conduct pillaging raids. The infantry each carried a large round shield and a heavy thrusting spear, like their Welsh opponents, but were rather less well equipped with protective jackets and helmets. A leather helmet reinforced with metal strips would be the best an Englishman could hope to own, unless he were royalty. Most men carried a heavy, single-bladed knife called a scramasax, which might be up to two feet long and could be murderous in close fighting.

English tactics were much simpler and less flexible than those of the post-Roman Welsh. With no cavalry, the English relied exclusively on an infantry tactic that was to become known as the shield-wall. The men formed up shoulder to shoulder and about seven or eight ranks deep. The men at the front held their shields forward, overlapping the edges so that, seen from the front, they did resemble a wall of shields. Usually the entire army formed a single shieldwall, and this seems to have been the case at Bindon.

When on the defensive, a shieldwall was positioned on top of a hill, behind hedges or along a stream, wherever offered the most protection. On the offensive, as at Bindon, the shieldwall was formed up so that each rank stood almost immediately on the heels of that in front. On a given signal, the mass of men began to move forward at a steady walking pace. The key to success was to keep a densely packed formation so that there was no opening for the Welsh cavalry to charge into and exploit. Bristling with spears and advancing at a steady pace, the shieldwall was an awesome tactic of war. It would simply roll over less well grouped formations and crush any poorly disciplined troops it met. And this seems to have been exactly what happened here.

Exactly where the English shieldwall struck the head of the advancing Dumnonian column we do not know. The heaviest fighting must have taken place at Bindon, which is the cluster of buildings about 300 yards beyond the road junction, for the battle was named after this hamlet.

Cynegils had chosen his spot carefully. The narrow valley is no place for the swooping, wheeling tactics of the Welsh cavalry, which would have been effectively useless. With the Dumnonian

◁ The charming waterfall outside the gates of Bindon Manor.

▽ The narrow nature of the valley just east of Bindon made this ideal infantry country and put the Dumnonian cavalry at a disadvantage.

A bench on the outskirts of Axmouth, provided by thoughtful locals for the use of walkers.

The lane back to Axmouth from Bindon passes some picturesque cottages.

infantry formed in column for the march, the crushing onslaught of the English shieldwall could meet and destroy each unit in turn.

Before long the Dumnonians were fleeing back down the valley towards the Axe.

6. Continue along the lane as it heads west down the valley to return to Axmouth and the starting point of the walk.

The flight of the Welsh was stopped by the tidal Axe, and it seems that many were caught and slaughtered on the English side of the river. When the fighting was over, the English counted the dead and found that they had killed 2,065 Dumnonians. The Dumnonian king was not among the dead, but Cynegils had no time to continue the pursuit. He had to head north to face the men of Gwent, probably somewhere near Frome. There was no major fighting, the King of Gwent conducting a prudent withdrawal once he realised that his ally had been crushed.

Thereafter Cynegils ruled for another thirty years, becoming a Christian in his old age. Most of his reign was devoted to efforts to bring the disparate parts of Wessex under centralized control. It would be left to his son (or possibly nephew, the records are not clear) King Cenwalh to face the Dumnonians again.

2. POSBURY
661

Distance:	1½ miles
Terrain:	Mostly over surfaced lanes with one steepish slope.
Public transport:	No public transport links to this battlefield.
Parking:	Some limited roadside parking, but care should be taken not to block the road to other motorists.
Refreshments:	No refreshment facilities on the walk, although plenty are available in Crediton three miles to the north-east.

After the crushing defeat of the Dumnonian invasion of Wessex at Bindon the two kingdoms were at comparative peace for a generation. No doubt there was a degree of border squabbling and there

The windblown trees that top the hill at Posbury. The walk passes along this lane on its way following what was probably the attack route taken by the West Saxons.

may have been battles the records of which have not survived, but there were no major wars.

But in 658 warfare erupted once again. King Cenwalh of the English kingdom of Wessex faced an invasion of the Welsh Dumnonians. He met the invaders at Penselwood, south of Frome. The Dumnonians received a crushing defeat and fled 'like a man flees fire', according to a contemporary account. The victory for Cenwalh was impressive and he was able to occupy most of Somerset as a result. Three years later he decided to continue the English advance into Dumnonia with a daring strike west past Exeter to surround and capture that city.

At the time Exeter was one of the largest and most prosperous cities in Britain, though given the basically agricultural nature of the economy that is not saying much. There were probably about

The view north-east from Posbury Camp. The Dumnonians manning the hillfort would have had a similar view of the route taken by the advancing West Saxons.

700 households in the city, giving a population of around 2,000. The city was still surrounded by its impressive Roman walls, sections of which still stand today, but defence depended on the Dumnonians mustering enough men into the city to man the defences. It was probably to stop this that Cenwalh found himself marching to Posbury, south-west of Crediton.

THE WALK

1. Follow the road from Crediton through the hamlet of Posbury to park where the road bends right and a track continues straight on up a steep hill.

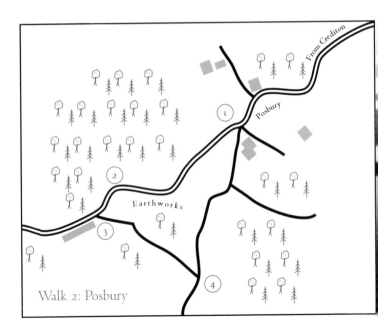

Walk 2: Posbury

Cenwalh and the Wessex army were advancing along this road. It seems that Cenwalh was making a major effort with this invasion of his neighbour, so his army may have been as much as 5,000 men strong. Neither weapons nor tactics had changed much since the Battle of Bindon, but the task facing Cenwalh at Posbury was very different. At Bindon King Cynegils had ambushed a Welsh army on ground of his choosing. Now Cenwalh had to dislodge his enemy from prepared defences.

2. Follow the lane south-west up the hill. The lane bends to the right then turns sharp left.

On the left of the lane stretches a field in which can be seen the banks and ditches of ancient earthworks. These are the remnants of

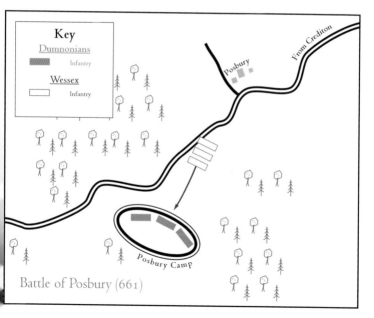

Battle of Posbury (661)

The earthworks of Posbury Camp are on private land that is not accessed by a footpath. They can, however, be clearly seen from the tracks used on this walk.

Posbury Camp, a pre-Roman hillfort that had been refortified by the Dumnonians in the post-Roman period. The exact nature of the renovations is not clear, but probably consisted of erecting a wooden palisade on the top of the banks and ensuring the ditch sides were steep and lacked any convenient footholds.

Details of exactly what happened here are unclear. The English certainly stormed these defences, pushing the Dumnonians back and capturing the hilltop.

3. Turn left along a surfaced track that runs behind the defensive earthworks, which come into view again to the left.

4. At a T-junction, turn left along a second track to return to the start of the walk.

The tracks used by this walk to circuit Posbury Camp are surfaced with gravel and stones, but can still be muddy in wet weather.

Having driven off the Dumnonian force, Cenwalh was in a position to block any reinforcements reaching Exeter to man its defences effectively. He must have thought that the campaign was as good as won, but he calculated without Dumnonian diplomacy. Even as he was marching on Exeter, Cenwalh learned that King Wulfhere of Mercia had invaded Wessex in response to Dumnonian pleas for help. Cenwalh hurried home, only to meet defeat at the hands of the Mercians. Wulfhere imposed harsh peace terms, removing territory from Wessex and ravaging other areas.

Cenwalh died in 672 having achieved something in the way of rebuilding his kingdom, though the chroniclers recorded as the most noteworthy event of his reign a great and sudden mortality of birds across Britain. In 682 his son and successor Centwine again invaded Dumnonia, this time without Mercian interference. He

The route back to the start of the walk from Posbury Camp goes down this steep section of track.

The English warriors who fought at Bindon and Posbury went to battle dressed in their usual farming clothes, but with the addition of a large round shield, heavy spear and a sidearm of some kind, here a sword. Only the richest men could afford a mail shirt or metal helmet.

won a great victory at an unknown location east of the Exe, marching on to occupy most of Devon as a result. Exeter surrendered without a fight.

Thereafter Dumnonia was restricted to the lands west of the Tamar where it became known by the name of its ruling dynasty: Cornwall. Cornwall was eventually absorbed by Wessex in about 875 as the two kingdoms came together to face the greater threat of the Vikings.

3. LYDFORD
997

Distance:	1 ½ miles.
Terrain:	Mostly over well-maintained footpaths or lanes; however, one section along an unsurfaced track can be muddy.
Public transport:	First Bus route 86 runs to Lydford from Okehampton.
Parking:	Small car park at the southern end of the village where the walk starts and finishes.
Refreshments:	The walk passes one pub which serves meals and bar snacks.

In 997 that most unfortunate of kings, Ethelred the Unready, had been on the throne of England for nineteen miserable years. He had come to the throne in murky circumstances following the murder of his popular half-brother Edward. Ethelred had only been a child at the time, a puppet of powerful nobles, but he never really recovered from the way he gained the throne. Combined with a talent for choosing incompetent officials and a knack for annoying people, the distrust engendered by Edward's death meant that Ethelred was rarely in a position to achieve much.

The Vikings sensed the weakness of Ethelred's regime and descended on England. Ethelred tried fighting, then he tried bribery and diplomacy. Nothing worked, for there was simply too much plunder to be had for little effort. Finally, in 997 the Vikings came to Devon.

We do not know who led the force of raiders who came to Devon late that summer. It may have been Swein Harroldson, a leading Danish prince whom we know to have been active at about this time. Whoever led them, the Vikings followed a strategy of swift, lightning moves. They landed to raid and plunder as much territory as possible within a few days, dashing back to their ships to get away before the local armed militia, or fyrd, could be summoned. They

The battle monument at Lydford, made by a local craftsman and paid for by the Women's Institute. It stands besidee the road entering Lydford, opposite the church.

As semi-professional fighters, the Vikings that attacked Lydford were well equipped by the standards of the day. Most men would have had a mail shirt, while all came equipped with helmet, shield and throwing javelins, as well as a primary weapon such as an axe or sword.

began in Cornwall in the spring, then moved north to attack the coasts of southern Wales before moving east to Watchet in Somerset, where they stayed for longer than usual. Some time around August they put out to sea again and disappeared over the horizon.

Moving out of sight of land the Danes headed around Land's End and then made a strike at the Tamar Valley. The landing achieved surprise and success. The villages were entirely unprepared and the Vikings captured huge amounts of livestock, newly harvested crops and cash. They then moved up the Tamar, pillaging as they went.

Despite the incompetence of its royal government at this time, England was not entirely defenceless. A century earlier Alfred the Great had defeated an earlier and much more powerful Viking threat by efficient use of the existing military systems of England and the introduction of dramatic reforms. These were still in place and, as the Danes moved up the Tamar Valley, the men of Devon put them into effect.

The key to the defence system was the burgh, a fortified town or village. The walls of these strongholds were maintained by the men of the surrounding villages, whose taxes paid for materials and whose forced labour kept the fortifications in good repair. As soon as danger threatened the villagers had to move themselves, their families and everything they owned to the nearest burgh. In theory no village should be further than a day's walk from a burgh, though this was not always the case.

For fighting men the English relied upon the fyrd, for which each village was expected to provide a certain number of men. The families clubbing together to afford the weaponry and armour demanded by the king, and a young man being chosen to go off to war as occasion demanded. These men were equipped in similar fashion to those who had fought at Bindon and Posbury, though the greater wealth of tenth-century England meant that more men could afford mail coats and quality arms than before.

The traditional system had been caught unawares by the sudden attack of the Vikings, but it was now swinging into action. The burgh protecting the upper Tamar Valley was Lydford. In 997 this was a small town, more important for the fact that the king's courts of justice and local government were based here than for any mercantile wealth or great population. The town was positioned on the north bank of the River Lyd, where a small tributary enters the river. The angle between the two water courses formed a steep-sided hill which dropped sheer on two sides, with a mighty earth and timber fortification on the third side.

As the Danes advanced, the locals poured into Lydford, driving their livestock before them and bringing in lumbering wagons loaded with the harvest. By the time the Vikings arrived the town was packed with refugees and their wealth, while the walls bristled with armed men.

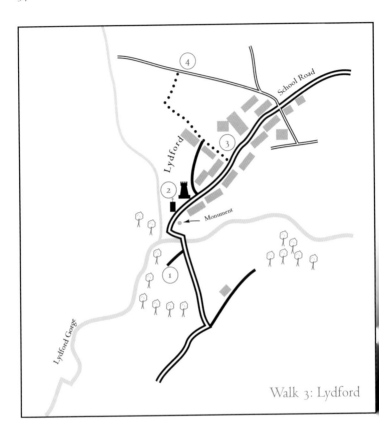

Walk 3: Lydford

THE WALK

1. From the car park that serves the Lydford Gorge, a beauty spot owned by the National Trust, walk north along the lane to pass over the gorge by way of a bridge. It is worth paying to visit the gorge properly, but if not you can catch a glimpse of this natural wonder from this bridge. The defensive properties of the gorge are obvious.

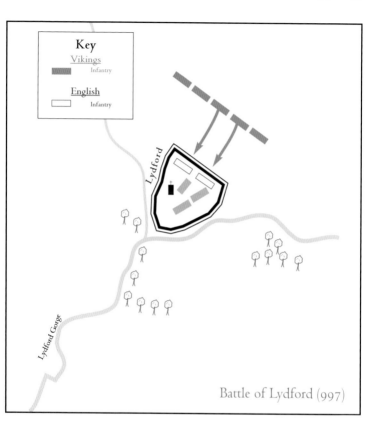

Battle of Lydford (997)

It was along this River Lyd that the Vikings advanced on that late summer's day of 997. They had been marching through an empty landscape from which all humans and farm animals had fled. They would have known from experience that the English had fled to a burgh. Whether they were following the tracks of the refugees or already knew where Lydford was we do not know.

The advancing host numbered something around 4,000 men, a sizeable army for its day. No doubt some of the men had been left

The depths of Lyford Gorge. The sheer-sided cleft is one of the natural wonders of Devon. The depth of the gorge can be seen from two figures to the top left of the photograph. The gorge loops around Lydford, which at the time of the attack made it effectively impossible to approach on two sides.

at the Tamar to guard the ships on which the safety of the Vikings depended, and others may have been out raiding or scouting, but it remains likely that some 3,000 Vikings were approaching Lydford.

These men were hardened warriors more accustomed to fighting than their English foes. They had been working together for some months and were a compact, cohesive force that could be relied upon to fight in disciplined and effective manner. The weaponry of the Vikings was not so very different from that of the English, though there were a few key distinctions.

Most Vikings went raiding equipped with a round wooden shield, metal helmet and most had a mail shirt. Most men carried a pair of javelins, which were thrown at the enemy to open the battle, and a heavy thrusting spear for close combat. The majority of men also had either a sword or axe as a secondary weapon. A few men carried the terrifying Danish axe that so impressed and appalled the English. This weapon had a haft some 5 feet long and a curved blade some 10 inches across. In action the weapon was kept in constant motion, the blade swooping and sweeping in great arcs to build up momentum. A skilled man could change the blade's direction in a flash, bringing the weapon down to deal out sudden death. It could slice through mail with ease and could hack a man in half. One Viking axeman was reputed to have killed forty Englishman in a single day with this awful weapon. Its use required not only great skill and enormous strength but also constant practice, so few men wielded it in battle.

2. From the Lyd, climb steeply up to the village. At the top of the slope you will find the church and castle to your left and the battle monument to your right.

In 997 this spot was occupied by one of only two gates into the fortified burgh. The rest of the perimeter was protected by timber palisades and fortifications. The slope made the defences effectively invulnerable to a force of infantry marching with only light equipment. The Vikings were looking for an easier approach, and they were soon to find it.

3. After exploring the church and castle, and finding the Viking rune stone left by a twentieth-century visitor from Scandinavia, continue along the lane. Pass The Castle pub and the post office. Then glance to your left into a field beside the village hall to see what remains of the English fortifications of 997. The earthen mound may not look too impressive now, but it would have been steeper and larger in 997 and topped by a timber wall. At a crossroads turn left, then bear left at a Y-junction. Continue on for 150 yards to find a footpath turning left.

It was about here that the Danes formed up to attack Lydford. In front of them was a smooth grassy slope down to the defences that guarded the easy approach to the town. These took the form of a 6-foot-deep ditch backed by an earthen rampart on top of which was a stout timber wall some 10 feet high. As with all burgh defences, it was designed to hold off a band of Viking raiders until the fyrd of the entire county could be mustered and march to aid the defenders. The English had to hold out for several days to be certain of safety.

The challenge for the Vikings was to get into the fortress before the county army arrived – which meant gaining the victory within a day or two at most. The usual tactic was to stage a demonstration of frightful power, then demand surrender.

The Viking army would have drawn up for battle with their weapons drawn and brandished. War songs would have been sung and chants shouted out. Flags were waved and formations of men

△ Lydford Castle dates to the medieval period, but is a well-preserved ruin and well worth a visit. It is now in the care of English Heritage.

▷ The interior of the keep of Lydford Castle. The floors and roof have long since vanished, but the enlarged windows and doors date from the Tudor period, when this was a major administrative building for the local justice system.

△ The church at Lydford is medieval, but stands on the site of the old English church that stood here on the day of the battle.

◁ The 1,000th anniversary of the battle of Lydford was marked by an official visit by men from Scandinavia. They brought with them this modern replica of a Viking runestone, which they left just outside the churchyard as a symbol of the modern goodwill that has replaced ancient enmity.

marched back and forth to display their might and discipline to the enemy. If any local Englishmen had been captured, they would be dragged forward and threatened with instant death. After having put on as good a demonstration as possible, the Vikings would have sent forward messengers to demand surrender or, more likely, a hefty cash payment to buy safety for the burgh. More than one English commander was so overawed that he paid up rather than face an assault by the notoriously ruthless Vikings. The defender of Lydford was made of sterner stuff: he refused even to talk to the Danes.

4. Follow the footpath over the open fields, turning sharp left to pass to the left of a line of cottages and so emerge into Lydford High Street. The English defences are to your left.

The Vikings would have surged forward from the north in a dense mass behind a solid line of interlocked shields. While some men hurled javelins at the defenders to keep them sheltering behind the wooden palisades, other Vikings dashed forward to leap over the ditch and attack the walls with axes. It was dangerous work, but effective. More than one such set of defences had fallen to this type of combined assault.

But not this time. The English defenders fought back with determination and skill. Arrows and spears were hurled at the main Viking host while other missiles rained down on those trying to demolish the walls. The fighting was fierce, but over quickly. The Viking commander soon pulled his men back. He realised that he would not take Lydford quickly and must have been nervous to be so far from his ships at a time when the Devon county fyrd was known to be gathering against him.

The Vikings gathered up their wounded, then turned away and marched back down the valley of the Lyd to their waiting ships.

△ The defences of the English burgh took the form of a wooden wall atop a steep bank behind a ditch. The rounded remains of the earthworks can be traced quite clearly on the eastern side of Lydford. It was about this spot, just north of the main gate, that the main Viking assault most probably took place.

◁ The Lydford Sundial stands outside the village hall.

They got there unmolested and headed for Tavistock. The monastery of Tavistock was burnt to the ground and everything of value stolen. The Vikings then moved on to the mouth of the Tamar where they fortified a convenient headland, possibly Torpoint. They had gathered enough food to keep them through the coming winter. The men of Devon approached the Viking base, but chose not to attack. A guard was put to watch the enemy over the winter while the rest of the fyrd went home. The campaign would begin again the following year.

5. Turn right along Lydford High Street. This area formed the heart of the fortified burgh in 997. There were few permanent buildings for open land was needed on which the livestock could be kept and refugees could camp. Pass the church, a medieval building occupying the site of the ninth-century original, and the medieval castle. Follow the lane back over the Lyd to return to the car park.

▷ *From Point 4 the walk returns to the centre of the village by way of this track, which can be muddy after rain.*

4. PINHOE
1001

Distance:	2 miles.
Terrain:	This walk runs over lanes and has only one stretch over open land where conditions may be muddy. There is a short but steep hill to be negotiated, but the going is not unduly difficult.
Public transport:	Pinhoe is now a suburb of Exeter and has its own railway station, where the walk starts and finishes.
Parking:	On-street parking in Pinhoe.
Refreshments:	The walk passes one pub which serves meals and bar snacks.

After being repulsed, but not defeated, at Lydford in 997 the Norwegian Vikings spent the winter in a fortified camp at the mouth of the Tamar. Rather than face the Devon militia they then headed east to continue with their strategy of moving quickly to strike at unprepared areas before making off in their ships and avoiding any local armies which could be mustered.

In 998 the Norwegians attacked Dorset and the Isle of Wight, in 999 they plundered Kent and in 1000 contented themselves with living off food and beer extorted under threat of violence in East Anglia. They began the campaigning season of 1001 by attacking Hampshire. A battle was fought at Dean, where the Vikings killed eighty-one Englishmen, including the county's High Reeve, Leofwine. Although the English fled, the Vikings had suffered losses and chose to get out while they could. In around July they returned to Devon.

This time they did not raid the valley of the Tamar, but instead landed at Exmouth. There they constructed a fortified base where their beached ships could be securely guarded against the Devon men. Only then did the Vikings begin their raiding.

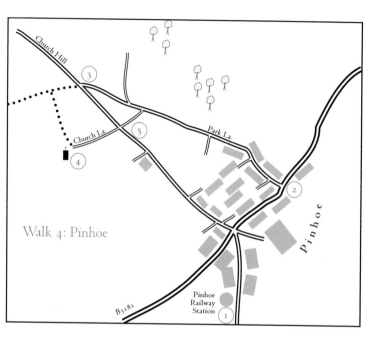

The first strike was successful. A force of Vikings went by sea to the River Teign, rowing up the broad estuary to reach the fortified town, or burgh, of Teingnton, now Kingsteignton. The attack achieved total surprise, the burgh being taken and burned without trouble. The Vikings moved on to loot and burn surrounding villages and manors for several days without interference.

On their return to base the Vikings found a force of ships approaching along the coast from the east. The ships were filled with armed men and the two fleets approached each other warily. The newcomers turned out to be a force of Danish mercenaries commanded by the famed Viking raider Pallig Tokesen, who was married to Gunhild, the sister of King Sweyn Forkbeard of Denmark, with whom Ethelred had a treaty of friendship. Sweyn

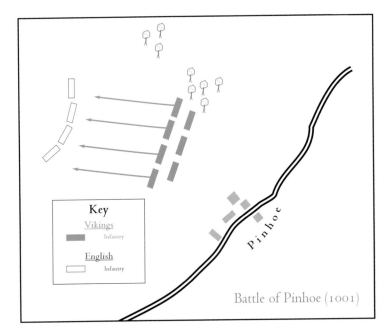

Battle of Pinhoe (1001)

claimed overlordship of Norway and was engaged in a long-running feud with King Olaf of Norway so there was little friendship between Pallig and the Norwegians.

This Pallig and his men had been hired by England's King Ethelred the Unready and given the task of cruising off the southern coasts of England to protect them against the hit and run tactics favoured by the Danes. Ethelred was presumably of the opinion that he should set a thief to catch a thief but, as so often, he proved to be a poor judge of character.

Although Ethelred had paid Pallig in cash, and given him a comfortable manor on which to live, he chose to join the Norwegians instead of fighting them. The size of the combined Viking force is not entirely clear, but was probably around 4,000 or

5,000 men all told. Feeling emboldened by the newcomers, the Viking force rowed up the River Exe to attack the wealthy city of Exeter.

The city was, however, ready for the attack. It was still surrounded by its Roman walls, which had been kept in good repair over the centuries since the legions had left. As soon as the Vikings had arrived the inhabitants of the nearby villages had, according to the usual English plan for local defence, fled to the city taking with them all their livestock and valuables. The walls were now manned by the men of the area. The Vikings, as usual, mounted a display of their armed might and then demanded instant surrender or payment of tribute. The defenders refused. Unable to do much against stone walls, the Vikings clambered back into their ships and returned to their base at Exmouth.

The invaders next move was to begin a determined and thorough sacking of the Exe Valley. The livestock and moveable wealth of the area might have been safe inside Exeter, but the buildings, standing crops and various amounts of tools and equipment were not. The Vikings spread out and moved north from Exmouth methodically destroying everything they could find but could not carry off as loot. Topsham went up in flames, so did Clyst St Mary. Then the Vikings moved on to Pinhoe, a small village just north-west of Exeter. It came as something of a shock to find the county army of Devon mustered just outside the village.

THE WALK

1. **What in 1001 was a small rural village is now a suburb of Exeter that grew up in Victorian times around the railway station built on the main line from Exeter to London. The**

walk begins and ends at the station. From the station walk north along Station Road to the junction with Main Road, the B3181. Turn right at the curious double mini roundabout.

This was roughly the route taken by the Vikings as they marched north. The English army was almost certainly gathered on Beacon Hill to the north. From this naturally defensive position they could look south over the Clyst Valley up which the Vikings were advancing. If the invaders chose to push deeper into Devon the English could cut them off from their base. Clearly the Vikings needed to defeat the Devon county army if they were to gain anything much from their stay in the area. They paused to loot Pinhoe and set fire to the buildings, then sat down to eat a meal before pushing on to face the English in battle.

2. After following Main Road for about 200 yards, turn left into Park Lane, passing the aptly named Saxon Close on the left and pushing steadily uphill for about 1,000 yards toward Beacon Hill.

3. Where Park Lane meets Church Hill, cross straight over to join a footpath that heads west across the hillside. After about 150 yards turn left along a second footpath towards a church with a tower.

It was somewhere on this open hillside above the Clyst that the Battle of Pinhoe was fought. Details of the fighting are scarce, though it is possible to reconstruct the outline of what happened.

The English had been camped on the hilltop, perhaps trusting to the strength of the position to deter an attack. In terms of numbers we do not know how many Englishmen were present. However they were led by the High Reeve for Devon, Kola, and

The Pinhoe walk starts and finishes at the railway station, served by frequent trains on the Exeter–London route.

his deputy Eadsige was also present. This would indicate that the main army for Devon was assembled.

There were, at this date, around 8,000 families for taxation purposes in Devon. These could probably put into the field some 2,000 properly equipped warriors who had some form of training for battle. In theory all men were liable for military service in local defence, but it was probably the more select fyrd, or militia, that were present at Pinhoe. Some of these men would have been on duty elsewhere, not least on the walls of Exeter, but even so some 1,500 English warriors must have been there on the day of battle.

This means that the English were outnumbered perhaps two to one by the Vikings. The Vikings had the advantage not only of numbers but also of being better trained and more used to battle as

Once out of the built-up area of Pinhoe the walk climbs steeply up this lane towards the parish church.

Having crossed Church Hill the walk passes between these two pillars to follow a footpath to the summit of the hill.

well as forming a coherent unit that had been together for some years of campaigning.

The Vikings attacked uphill without hesitation and, although details are lacking, they seem to have been successful in their first charge. The English fought well, but they eventually gave way and fled back toward the safety of the walls of Exeter. Neither of the English commanders was killed. This would indicate that the withdrawal was made in good order as the death or capture of enemy leaders was usually a key ambition of a Viking army.

Although they won the day – 'The heathens had the power of the battlefield', as one contemporary chronicle puts it – they gained little. As soon as the battle was over they returned to their ships at Exmouth. Within days the temporary alliance broke up. Pallig led his ships hurriedly east to London to make his peace with King

Looking back to the summit of the hill from the churchyard. The defending English army was almost certainly positioned in or close to this field while the Vikings attacked uphill towards them.

Ethelred while the Norwegians moved to the Isle of Wight where they established a new fortified camp for the winter.

It must be presumed that although they lost the battle, the men of Devon had inflicted such losses as to cause the Vikings to leave the county.

4. At the church turn left along Church Lane. This runs down the slope to Church Hill.

5. Turn right to walk down the hill to reach Main Road. Return along Station Road to the railway station and the start of the walk.

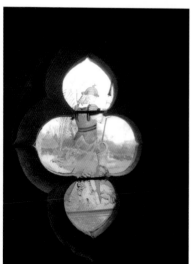

△ The church at Pinhoe stands just south of the likely site of the battle. The location may have been chosen to identify the site of the burial pits where the Christian English dead were interred.

◁ The porch of Pinhoe church has a suitably martial stained-glass window. St George is shown standing triumphant over the dragon, a scene commonly used to depict Christianity's triumph over paganism.

5. EXETER CASTLE
1136

Distance:	1 mile.
Terrain:	Well-maintained footpaths or lanes.
Public transport:	Exeter is well served by rail and bus routes. The walk starts and ends at Exeter Central station.
Parking:	Several well-signed car parks in the city centre and the castle.
Refreshments:	Numerous pubs, cafés and snack shops in the city centre.

The Roman walls around the city of Exeter were built in around 275 to defend the city as barbarian attacks on the empire began to become more frequent and increasingly dangerous. They were improved in the final years of imperial control and maintained with enthusiasm by the citizens of Exeter through the troubled years that followed.

So effective were the walls that they were never taken by force. Only starvation or treachery ever opened the gates of the city. It was perhaps for this reason that William the Conqueror decided to build a castle inside them. When he reached Exeter in 1068 he found the city gates closed against him. The citizens were concerned not only for their own safety, but also that of Gytha, mother of the King Harold who was killed at the Battle of Hastings in 1066, and his children who lived in the city. Only after they had got away to Ireland in a fishing boat did the city surrender. William wanted a bastion within the city walls on which he could depend. He therefore tore down several houses on a knoll of red rock in the northern angle of the old Roman walls and built in their place a mighty castle that was named Rougemont, or Red Mount from the knoll on which it stood.

In the decades that followed the original castle was improved and strengthened several times. The gate acquired a barbican, an outwork designed to block any attempt at a surprise attack, while the curtain

An infantryman equipped in typical war gear for the time of the siege. He wears a metal helmet, but is otherwise unarmoured. His wooden shield is edged with metal and has an iron boss that covers the handgrip. He carries a thrusting spear as his main weapon, but would probably have had a heavy hunting knife as well.

walls were strengthened and the mighty Athelstan's Tower added to cover a blind spot where the castle walls met the old Roman city walls. It was by 1136 the epitome of modern military engineering. The importance of the fortress was emphasised by the fact that successive kings of England had kept it in royal ownership, never granting it to a feudal vassal.

It was therefore with some concern that King Stephen received a visit from a dusty and dishevelled burgher of Exeter in the spring of 1136. The man carried an urgent message from the city council complaining of the behaviour of the castle's commander Sir Baldwin Redvers. This Sir Baldwin was holding the castle on behalf of the king, but unusually for a man holding such a castle was also a wealthy landowner and leading baron in his own right.

The citizens complained that Sir Baldwin was disturbing the king's peace by commandeering food and supplies in excess of the customary amounts and not making proper payment. To all appearances he was preparing for a war.

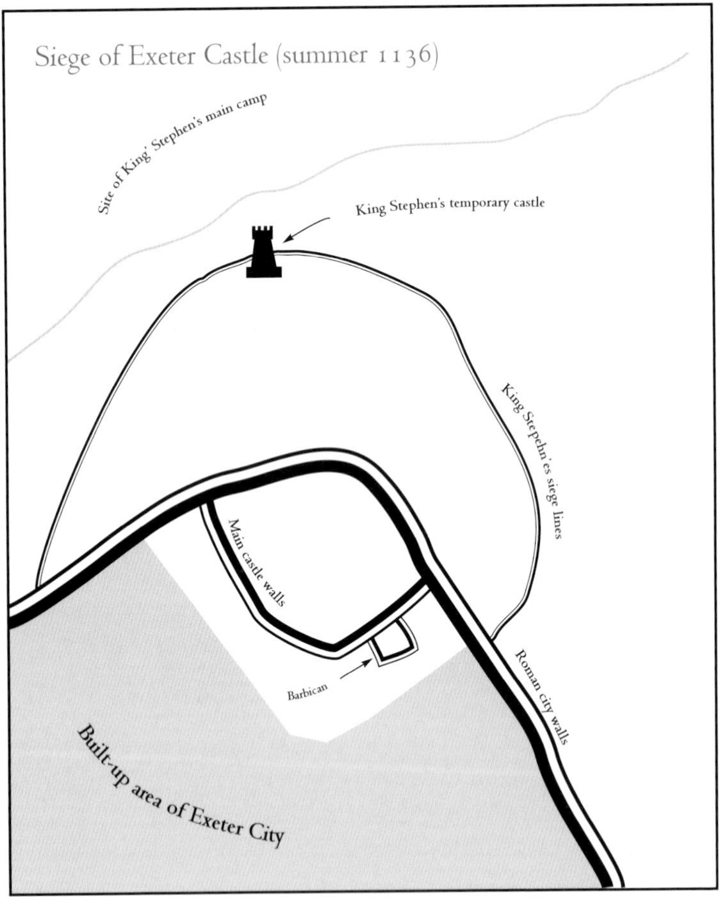

Siege of Exeter Castle (summer 1136)

Site of King Stephen's main camp

King Stephen's temporary castle

King Stephen's siege lines

Main castle walls

Barbican

Roman city walls

Built-up area of Exeter City

King Stephen had good reason to be disturbed. He had not been on the throne for a year and his grip on power was shaky to say the least. The previous king, Henry I, had left the crown to his daughter, Matilda. But she had been in France when Henry died, and Stephen moved quickly. He was the dead king's nearest male

King Stephen's knights who rode to Exeter to investigate rumours of rebellion would have been equipped in a similar fashion to this figure. He has a mail shirt and mail trousers together with a flat-topped helmet of iron. His shield is of wood painted with a heraldic device, repeated on the helmet, that identifies the man.

relative, he was tall, handsome and charming, and he was a good soldier. First one nobleman then another declared for Stephen, claiming as a pretext for ignoring Matilda an arcane feudal duty that she had overlooked. On 22 December 1135, Stephen was crowned King of England.

Almost at once the trouble began. Henry I had spent years stripping the barons of powers and privileges that made them too powerful. Now they began demanding them back as the price for supporting Stephen. Stephen delayed giving a straight answer. Among those making the most noise was Sir Baldwin Redvers.

So when Stephen received the messenger from Exeter he moved fast. At the time he was in Oxfordshire with a small army dealing with Sir Robert of Bampton, a knight who had raided some land of his neighbours to get money to pay off his debts. Although he was in the midst of a siege, the king detached 200 of his finest soldiers and sent them riding hard for Exeter with orders to dismiss Sir Baldwin from his command of the castle.

The armoured horsemen travelled swiftly, arriving at Exeter before anyone expected them. They rode through the gates, ignoring the challenges of Sir Baldwin's guards, and headed for the castle. Sir Baldwin was not there, but his wife Adelise was. Seeing armed horsemen galloping through the city streets she immediately guessed who had sent them and on what mission. She ordered the castle gates to be slammed shut.

Lady Adelise then appeared on the parapet of the gatehouse. In reply to the challenge to surrender to the king's authority, she replied that her husband had charged her to hold the castle until his return and that she would open the gates to nobody else. The royal troops retired to watch the castle and sent a rider off to inform Stephen of events. Perhaps the most interesting feature of this exchange is not simply that a woman could take command of a castle and its military garrison, but that nobody seemed to think this at all unusual or worthy of comment.

As soon as Bampton had been dealt with, Stephen marched to Exeter. He sent a small force off to Sir Baldwin's castle at Plympton to see if he was there. He wasn't, so the soldiers took the garrison prisoner and burned the castle to the ground before continuing on to rejoin Stephen at Exeter.

The king, meanwhile, had arrived at Exeter with his army. He personally demanded that Lady Adelise surrender the royal castle to him, but was rebuffed. The siege began in earnest.

THE WALK

1. From Exeter Central railway station, walk north along Queen Street. Cross over the B3183, North Road, at a roundabout which has a clock tower at its centre, and into Elm Grove to reach Howell Road. Turn right. After about 200 yards turn left

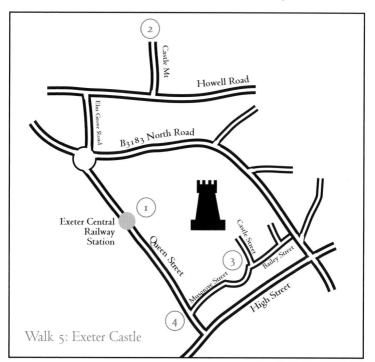

Walk 5: Exeter Castle

△ The modern reservoir in Castle Mound is flanked by these earthen slopes on which bushes grow. The temporary siege castle built by King Stephen stood on this spot.

▷ The clock tower that dominates the roundabout at the foot of Elm Grove.

into the cul-de-sac Castle Mound. On the right can be seen a reservoir built in the early twentieth century.

This area of Exeter, north of the railway lines, was developed in Victorian times as the need for housing caused the urban area of the city to spread out beyond its old city walls. In 1136 this was a broad valley through which a stream meandered. The meadows were prone to winter floods so they were kept under grass and grazed by herds of cattle and sheep. Immediately north of the valley was a small, steep hill on which the university has now been built.

King Stephen camped his army on the far side of the small stream, on the lower slopes of the hill. On the southern side of the stream he ordered his men to erect a temporary siege castle to block any exit from the castle on this side. The castle took the form of a wooden tower set on an earthen mound and surrounded by a wooden palisade. A stout wooden fence was built from the old Roman walls in a loop to enclose completely the area overlooked by the castle walls.

These impressive works were allowed to fall into ruin after the siege, but the main earthworks withstood the test of time until swept away to make room for the reservoir. Only the name of this road keeps their memory alive.

2. Return south along Castle Mound to Howell Road. Turn right and return to the North Road roundabout. Turn left into North Road, the B3183. Follow this road for about 400 yards, then follow it round to the right and over the railway line. Immediately over the bridge you will find the extensive park of Northenhay Gardens on your right. Continue south along New North Road for 350 yards, then turn right into Bailey Street.

This street marks the site of the open ground that was kept between the castle walls and the first city houses. Such an open area was essential to guard against a surprise attack launched by enemies who crept up under cover of the houses. It also served as an open area that any attackers had to cross and on which they would be vulnerable to arrow fire.

Stephen evacuated the houses on the south side of Bailey Street of their inhabitants and instead filled them with his soldiers. They had orders to shoot anyone who tried to enter or leave the castle. Stephen was determined that neither food nor men would get in or out of the castle.

But he was not content merely to wait for the garrison to starve. After all, the loyal citizens of Exeter had told him of the vast stocks of food that the elusive Sir Baldwin had packed into the fortress. It promised to be a long wait, and Stephen did not want to waste time while other barons were getting restive.

A siege engine was constructed and dragged into position in front of the castle gates. This was probably a trebuchet, a sling that was worked on a lever principle. It was a tall, narrow machine ideal for use in a street. The trebuchet could hurl a rock weighing several hundred weight over 150 yards. That put it outside the range of arrows shot from the castle. The rock followed a high, arcing trajectory so that it fell almost vertically down into the castle. It was not designed to smash the defensive walls so much as to make life uncomfortable and dangerous for those sheltering behind them.

3. At the eastern end of Bailey Street, turn right into Castle Street and enter Northernhay Gardens.

The stones hurled by the trebuchet seemed to be having little effect, so Stephen sent for a team of miners and ordered them to tunnel under the castle walls and bring them down. Given the fact

◁ The towering gatehouse of Exeter Castle is the most impressive of the remains to be seen today in Northernhay Gardens. It was from here that the rebels defied King Stephen.

▽ One of the cannon preserved at Exeter Castle. These guns date from several centuries after the siege.

△ The scenic Northernhay Gardens
in which stand the ruins of Exeter
Castle. The dip seen here is the
remnant of the moat that originally
surrounded the castle. The ruins are
behind the trees to the right.

▷ The section of city wall that forms
the northern defences of the castle. The
lower part of the wall is Roman, the
upper sections a medieval rebuilding.

that the castle was built on an outcrop of solid sandstone, the miners did not get very far. After a month of tunnelling they had to report that it would take almost as long to undermine the walls as it would to starve the garrison.

Stephen now turned to fire as a weapon. He sent for supplies of pitch to make fire arrows and ordered his archers to shoot them over the castle walls in the hope of hitting the thatched roofs of the domestic buildings beyond. This proved to be a highly successful ruse and soon many of the structures within the walls were roofless shells. The blisteringly hot weather of the summer of 1136 aided the fire attacks.

Finally, after almost three months, the garrison shouted out that they wanted to send out messengers to discuss surrender terms with the king. A truce was arranged and two of Sir Baldwin's leading officers came out. They were led through the city to the king's tent outside the walls and negotiations began. The key point of the talks was, at first, the whereabouts of Sir Baldwin Redvers. King Stephen wanted to lay hands on the rebel, while the garrison were equally anxious to know where he was and if he was coming to their aid.

A usual agreement under such conditions would be for the fighting to cease and for the garrison to agree to surrender by a certain date if no relieving force had arrived and driven off the besiegers. Given the huge stocks of food known to be in the castle such an agreement promised to name a date some weeks into the future and Stephen expected to have to make great concessions to get the date brought forward. It soon became clear, however, that Sir Baldwin's officers were quite happy to surrender almost at once given the right terms.

Stephen was puzzled by the tone of the negotiations, but his brother Bishop Henry of Winchester solved the riddle. He noticed that the cheeks of the two men were sagging badly – a clear sign of dehydration. Bishop Henry recalled the long, hot weather and at once concluded that the well inside the castle had run dry.

Left: *Athelstan's Tower has nothing to do with King Athelstan, since it was built some 400 years after the monarch's death. It was erected to strengthen the juncture between the castle walls on the right of this photograph and the city walls beyond. Right: The passage through Athelstan's Tower links the two parts of Northernhay Gardens.*

Pretending to lose interest in talks, King Stephen sent the men back to the castle to await developments. If Bishop Henry were correct a fresh offer of surrender would soon follow.

At dawn next day Lady Adelise herself appeared. She came barefoot with her hair hanging loose and wearing the simple gown of a pilgrim. Brought before King Stephen she threw herself at the king's feet and burst into tears. She begged for mercy for herself and the garrison, stating that she had merely been following her husband's orders and had never intended rebellion or treason. She agreed to surrender at once and declare undying loyalty to the king if allowed to surrender on generous terms.

Stephen treated the lady courteously, but firmly informed her that she and her men would have to surrender unconditionally. In other

This impressive statue of a deer hunter by Exeter-born artist B.B. Stephens dominates the northern entrance to Northernhay Gardens.

words their lives would be forfeit as rebels and Stephen would be free to execute them if he so chose. Lady Adelise was led back to the castle gates and pushed back inside.

As soon as she was gone uproar in the king's camp followed. Earl Robert of Gloucester, an illegitimate son of King Henry I and one of the richest noblemen in England, protested at the way the lady had been treated. He was joined by several other nobles who pointed out that the soldiers in the castle had only been following orders and so they should not be blamed for Sir Baldwin's crimes. Stephen countered that he was king and that all Englishmen should obey his orders, no matter what their employer had told them to do. The debate raged on for some hours. Finally Stephen gave way. He allowed Lady Adelise and her men to walk free from Exeter, taking with them anything they could carry in the way of money or arms.

The siege was over, but the fighting was not. Unknown to King Stephen, Robert of Gloucester and others were secretly in league with Sir Baldwin. They plotted to bring Matilda to England and to place her on the throne occupied by Stephen. Sir Baldwin had struck before the others were ready.

The rising was finally launched in 1138. It failed to oust Stephen, but successfully plunged England into years of civil war and anarchy. The main fighting took place outside Devon, but the lawlessness, chaos and bloodshed spilled over into the county. Thousands were killed, tens of thousands made homeless and millions had their lives disrupted and their goods stolen. In the words of a contemporary chronicler, 'this was a time when God and his angels slept'.

4. After exploring the castle ruins, leave the park by the gate through which you entered and walk south along Castle Street. Turn right into Musgrove Street. Follow this street to Queen Street. Turn right to return to Exeter Central railway station and the start of the walk.

6. EXETER CITY
1497

Distance:	1 mile.
Terrain:	City centre footpaths.
Public transport:	Well served by rail and bus services.
Parking:	Several car parks.
Refreshments:	Numerous pubs and cafes as well as shops selling snacks and soft drinks.

Devon escaped the various dynastic struggles and baronial uprisings of the Middle Ages relatively peacefully. There were no major sieges or battles in the county and the few skirmishes that did take place were so minor that nobody thought to record the sites where they had taken place. All that was to change in 1497.

In 1485 King Richard III, the last of the Plantagenets had been killed at the Battle of Bosworth in Leicestershire and replaced by King Henry VII, the first of the Tudors. However, Henry was not the closest heir to the throne. That honour lay with Edward and Richard, the young sons of King Edward IV who have become known to history as the Princes in the Tower. Henry put out the story that the boys had been murdered by Richard in 1483, but could produce no evidence to back up his claim. In fact, nobody really knew for certain what had happened to the missing boys.

In November 1491 a young man stepped off a ship in Cork, Ireland, accompanied by a group of exiled English noblemen. He announced that he was the missing Prince Richard who had been spirited out of England by relatives of his mother in 1483 at the age of nine to be brought up in secret exile in Flanders. Now he had come back to claim his rightful place as King of England and of Ireland.

△ Exeter Cathedral dominates the city centre. There was a Christian community in late-Roman times and the faith may have survived through the years of rule by the pagan kings of Wessex until the city was officially converted to the Christian faith in the seventh century. It is known that the present cathedral stands on the site of a much older church, but how old is unclear.

▷ A weathered stone knight, just one of dozens of medieval carvings on the west front of the catedral.

It later transpired that the boy had grown up as the son of a Flemish merchant named Werbecque and that he had been known in recent years as Pierrequin. He was quickly dubbed Perkin Warbeck by the supporters of King Henry and it is by that name that he is generally known today.

The years that followed Warbeck's arrival in Ireland were taken up by tortuous intrigues between Irish and English nobles, the crowned heads of Europe and assorted adventurers. Some members of the Plantaganet family recognised Warbeck as the missing Richard, others did not. He was recognised as King of England by King James IV of Scotland and housed in luxury in Edinburgh – until Henry VII sent an English army to invade Scotland.

By 1497 Henry's diplomacy, bribery and military threats had stripped Warbeck of his supporters. He was back in Ireland, living with the Earl of Desmond who was in rebellion against English overlordship. In the summer it became clear that Desmond would soon make peace with Henry and that Warbeck's arrest would be a condition of the treaty. The Irish lord advised Warbeck to leave while he could, and gave him enough gold to pay his travel expenses to some remote part of Christendom where he would be free of Henry's agents.

It was fateful that news arrived at that very moment of unrest in the south-west of England. Henry had introduced a new tax to pay for the Scottish war and, breaking tradition, had imposed it on the southern as well as the northern counties. Protests and riots broke out across Cornwall, Devon and Somerset, with royal officials being beaten up and sent packing. Hearing the news Warbeck decided to risk landing in England and spent his travel money hiring mercenaries. He had only enough money for 300 men and a short campaign, but he gambled on raising support and cash once in England.

On 7 September he landed at Whitesands Bay and headed straight for Exeter. On the way he collected some 3,000 local men at Bodmin and had some 6,000 men in all by the time he reached Exeter on 17 September.

THE WALK

1. At the cathedral, enter and find the high altar.

Warbeck was desperate to get to the high altar of Exeter Cathedral. Although he was calling himself King Richard IV of England, he had not yet been crowned. Tradition demanded that a

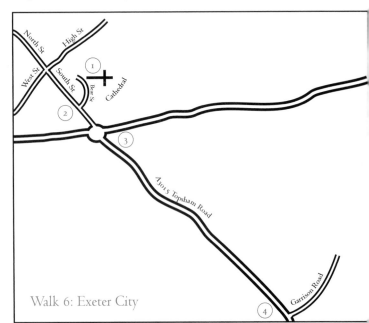

Walk 6: Exeter City

coronation had to take place in an English cathedral and, ideally, should be performed by the Archbishop of Canterbury. That cleric was far distant, but Warbeck had no doubt he could cajole some local priest into some form of temporary ceremony that would at long last add some form of divine legitimacy to his claim.

2. Exit the cathedral by the West Front and turn left along a pedestrianised alley named Bear Street to emerge into South Street. Turn left and follow this road downhill to the site of the old city gates.

The South Gate has long since been demolished to make access to the city centre easier, but an adjacent section of city wall

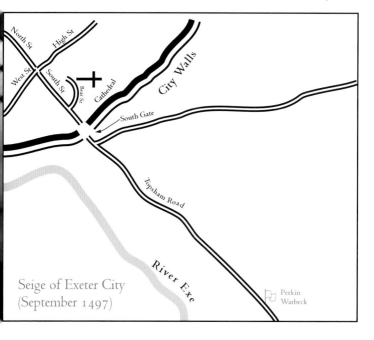

Seige of Exeter City
(September 1497)

is still standing and gives a good idea of the obstacle to be over-come by anybody trying to get into Exeter by force. The site of the former gate is marked by a plaque on a building, while the layout of the foundations is picked out in coloured brick on the ground.

Warbeck summoned the city to surrender here, but received a curt refusal from the city officials. Not only were they not inclined to join a rebellion, despite their opposition to the new tax, but they had a detachment of royal troops billeted in the city. These men would not only encourage loyalty, but could be relied upon to hold the walls with professional skill.

Balked of an easy surrender, Warbeck decided to lay siege to the city. By dawn on 18 September he had about 10,000 men camped outside the city walls, but neither he nor they had any guns or other siege equipment. Lacking the means to smash through the walls or undermine them, Warbeck was left with only two choices. He could order his men to scale ladders to get over the walls or he could organise an attempt to force the gates. It was the latter option that he chose.

Soon after sunset teams of men crept forward to attack the West Gate and South Gate, traditionally considered the weakest due to the lack of any natural obstacle on the approach. Covered by archers whose arrows were sent to pepper the battlements and so deter the defenders from retaliating, the main force was tasked with breaking down the gates. Those at the West Gate carried forester's axes and set to work to chop their way through the timber. Those at the South Gate carried bundles of kindling and firewood which they piled up against the gates and set alight.

At the West Gate the attackers sustained heavy loss and were driven off. At the South Gate the flames caught hold of the dry timber gates and a massive conflagration burst out that consumed not only the gates, but most of the gatehouse as well. Warbeck

◁ The walk passes these grand town houses on its way from the cathedral to South Street. During the siege the street would have been occupied by less imposing wooden houses.

▽ South Street looking from the site of South Gate towards the cathedral. The fiercest fighting took place in the foreground of the photograph.

The patterned brickwork in South Street marks the foundations of the original South Gate, now demolished.

began to marshal his followers to storm through the gateway once the flames had died down enough to allow passage.

The defenders had not been idle, however. Seeing the gate going up in flames they had torn up the cobblestones from South Street just inside the gateway. A deep pit was dug and sprinkled with sharpened wooden stakes, then backed by a makeshift wooden fence. They massed behind these defences to await the onslaught.

Soon after dawn on 19 September the flames were seen to be fading, so men were sent forward with iron hooks to drag aside the embers. As soon as the way was clear, Warbeck's men surged forward to storm into the city. They burst through the fallen gates to be confronted by the ditch, but got across and assaulted the fencing beyond. For almost an hour the fighting raged, but Warbeck's men could not get past the determined defenders.

A section of the city wall just west of the demolished South Gate. The wall survives to a height of about 16 feet at this spot, but at the time of siege was around 25 feet high.

By mid-morning Warbeck had called off the attack. Some 200 rebels and almost 100 loyalists lay dead around the southern end of South Street.

3. Continue straight across a roundabout along the A3015 Topsham Road for about 800 yards to the junction with Garrison Road.

Opinions differ as to Warbeck's position during the fighting. Certainly he was somewhere on the Topsham Road and may have been watching the assault from this small rise in the ground. The area between here and the city walls has now been built over, but in 1497 was open ground. It was here that he met his retreating troops. Realising that he would be unable to get into Exeter he

The broken end of the city wall beside South Gate shows the construction of the interior. A jumble of stones of various shapes have been rammed together and secured with mortar.

decided to march north-east to Taunton. He hoped that he could raise the Somerset men on the way and that he would be able to seize the armoury of Taunton Castle, and so would have siege equipment able to break into cities such as Exeter.

In the event neither happened. The failure to capture Exeter dispirited Warbeck's supporters, most of whom melted away to return home before reaching Taunton. Warbeck fled to seek sanctuary in a monastery and emerged only when he had received guarantees that his life would be spared. He was lodged in comfortable quarters in London, under constant armed guard, by Henry.

Suspicions soon grew that Warbeck was an illegitimate son of Edward IV, who was known to have been a great womaniser and moreover had met Warbeck's mother at about the right time for

A plaque commemorates the site of South Gate, demolished to allow for easier entry into the city of Exeter once peace and order made the fortifications unnecessary.

the young man to be his son. Certainly he bore a striking resemblance to Edward IV. In 1498 Warbeck escaped from London and tried to make for his boyhood home, but was caught before he could get out of England. Henry threw him into prison and, when a plot to use him as the figurehead for a revolt was discovered, ordered his execution.

Exeter was to be put under siege several other times, most notably during the Prayer Book Rebellion of 1549 and again – twice – in the Civil War of the 1640s. On each occasion the attackers chose to blockade the city rather than to attack so there was no real fighting.

4. Return back along the Topsham Road to South Street and so to the cathedral and the start of the walk.

7. FENNY BRIDGES
1549

Distance:	3¾ miles.
Terrain:	Mostly over surfaced lanes. However one section runs over open fields and may be muddy after rain.
Public transport:	Cook's Coaches bus route 382 runs to Fenny Bridges from Bowd.
Parking:	On-street parking in the village.
Refreshments:	The walk passes one pub which serves meals.

The religious wars of the sixteenth and seventeenth centuries between Catholics and Protestants largely passed England by. Perhaps the recent bloodletting of the Wars of the Roses dissuaded the English from civil conflict, or perhaps the skill of the Tudor monarchs in steering a moderate path ensured little conflict.

Whatever the case, there were some outbreaks of religious violence of which by far the most bloody took place in Devon during the summer of 1549. King Henry VIII had died in 1547 leaving as his heir the ten-year-old Edward VI. While Henry's Protestantism could be termed 'Catholicism without the Pope', Edward's was altogether a more radical and fiery faith. Under the guidance of his uncle, the Duke of Somerset, Edward approved a new Book of Common Prayer that set down which services were allowed to be performed in English churches. Crucially a new law was passed stating that only those services could be celebrated and that no local variations would be allowed. The new rites were clearly Protestant, banning the music and colourful ceremonies of Catholicism.

In Cornwall and Devon most people had been content with the old services and there was none of the fervour for Protestantism that held sway elsewhere in the country. It was unfortunate that the

The River Otter at Fenny Bridges. The wide stream has high, steep banks at this point, which made the possession of the bridges key to the battle. This view is from the modern bridge looking north.

The view east from the main bridge. It was along this road that the Royalist army advanced to battle.

The modern bridge at Fenny Bridges. At the time of the battle a much narrower bridge spanned the Otter in about the same location.

religious move coincided with a crisis of government finances that necessitated debasing the coinage of the realm and also with a crop failure. The new Prayer Book became the focus of opposition to the government of Somerset.

On Whit Sunday the parish priest of Sampford Courtney stood up to begin his service according to the new rites. Within minutes he had been set upon by his congregation who roughed him up, tore up his book and forced him to continue according to the traditional rituals. The news spread rapidly and the following Sunday the parishioners in most Devon churches likewise forced their priests to revert to the old practice.

At this point the staunchly Catholic Sir Humphrey Arundel, governor of St Michael's Mount, decided to make his move. He broke open the armoury of the castle of which he was in charge and announced that he was going to overthrow the hated government of Somerset. In fact he aimed at destroying Protestantism and imposing Catholicism on England, though this was kept secret from the discontented countrymen who flocked to his banner.

Arundel marched his men to Exeter, which closed its gates against him. Lacking siege equipment, Arundel decided to blockade the city and starve it into surrender. A few days later, a royal army arrived at Honiton led by Lord John Russell, an experienced commander. Russell had 4,000 men with him and although these were generally better trained than Arundel's 10,000 rebels they were not much better armed. Russell decided to try talking instead of fighting.

Russell rode down to Exeter with a guard of cavalry and asked exactly what it was that Arundel and his rebels wanted. Arundel replied by handing over a document containing fifteen articles. Taken together these would effectively have restored not just the old rituals but also Papal authority over England and Catholicism in all its force. Crucially one article called for all lands that had been taken by Henry VIII to be restored without compensation and another demanded that anyone who objected to the restored faith should be condemned as a heretic and executed as such. The first was clearly unacceptable to the cash-strapped government while the second proved to be highly unpopular with the populace.

Russell sent the demands off to London, together with a request for reinforcements of men and supplies. After some weeks a reply signed by Edward himself came back. It was a lengthy letter which rambled somewhat over the religious disputes of the day. The key passages were however short and simple. First, none of the fifteen articles was to be put into force by the government. Secondly a deadline of the end of July was put down for the rebels to disperse. Those who disarmed and went home by that date would receive free pardons, those who did not would be treated as traitors to be hunted down and killed.

Russell sent the reply on to Arundel and sat back at Honiton to await developments. Late on 25 July his scouts came riding in to report that almost half the rebel army was on the march towards Honiton. The offer of pardon had impressed few, there was to be a fight. Russell had no intention of waiting passively for the rebels to attack, so he ordered his own men to be ready to march in full battle order at dawn the next day.

THE WALK

1. In Fenny Bridges find the bridge over the River Otter and cross to the east bank.

The advance guard of Arundel's rebels had been sent to seize this strategic crossing point soon after dawn. They had crossed the river and positioned themselves defensively in the water meadows either side of the road before sitting down to rest. It was about mid-

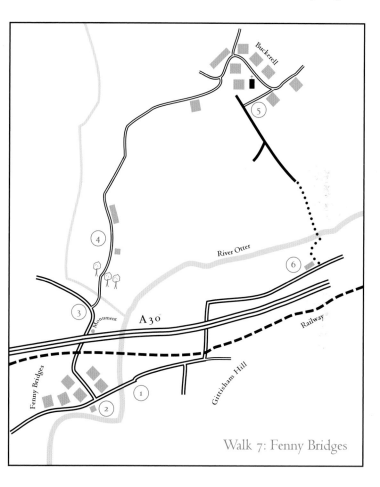

Walk 7: Fenny Bridges

morning when they saw the advance guard of Russell's army appear over the shoulder of Gittsham Hill to the east. The Victorian railway embankment now blocks this view, and the course of the road has been altered somewhat, though only in parts as we shall see later in the walk.

PRAYER BOOK REBELLION 1549
✕ FENNY BRIDGES ✕

HERE IN THIS MEADOW, ON 29TH JULY 1549
MEN FROM CORNWALL AND DEVON FOUGHT AND DIED
TO PRESERVE THEIR RELIGIOUS FAITH AND PRACTICE
AND THE LANGUAGE IN WHICH
THEY HAD BEEN BROUGHT UP.

OMMA YN DROLL-MA, AN 29AY MYS GORTHEREN 1549,
KERROW HA DEWNANS A OMLADWAS HA MERWEL
RAK MENTENA AGA FYTH HAGA USADOW CRYJYK
NEN YETH MAY FYENS-Y MEGYS

ERECTED 2000 BY THE HONITON HISTORY SOCIETY
AND KESKERDH KERNOW WITH HELP FROM
LOCAL COUNCILS AND SOCIETIES
AND THE ROAD CONTRACTORS

◁ The battle monument at Fenny
Bridges. The monument stands to the
north of the bridge to mark the location of
the Cornish archers during the battle.
The field beyond the monument is Blood
Meadow.

▽ The little bridge that carries the walk
over the stream beside Blood Meadow.
The rebels tried to stand here, but were
swept away by a renewed assault by
Royalists.

A messenger was sent galloping back over the bridge to alert Arundel and the main body of rebel troops. The Royalists, meanwhile, halted at about the spot where the road emerges from a bridge under the railway.

Arundel arrived quickly, while the rebel soldiers continued to arrive behind him. By noon the bulk of the Royalist army had also arrived and taken up position on Gittisham Hill facing down into the valley. Arundel studied the army facing him and decided to fight a defensive battle for control of the bridge over the Otter.

Arundel pulled his advance guard back over the bridge. He positioned the better armed of his 4,000 men to block the bridge and its immediate flanks. The less well armed farm labourers were put on the right flank where the Otter swept around to the west so as to delay any attempt by the Royalists to outflank the position. That left around 400 highly skilled Cornish archers equipped with the formidable longbow. Arundel placed them on his left flank where the river turned east. From this position they could pour arrows into the flank of any Royalist force advancing on the bridge while being protected by the river. The archers' position was just north of the railway line. Their position can no longer be seen from the bridge, but in 1549 the archers would have had an uninterrupted view over which to shoot.

At this date the conduct of battles was changing rapidly. Gunsmiths were for the first time producing guns that fired reliably in action, largely due to the production of improved gunpowder. The weapons were still cumbersome and heavy, needing to be supported on a stick set upright in the ground, and could fire only once every minute or so. In a straight exchange of fire they were no match for the longbow in terms of range or accuracy, but they were nonetheless increasingly effective. It was usual to position musketeers armed with these guns alongside halbardiers armed with swords as well as six foot long halbards and wearing helmets. The

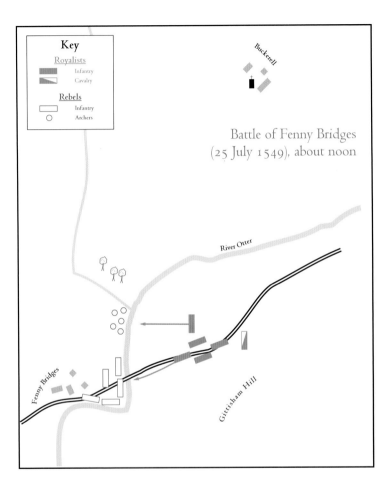

task of the halbardiers was to guard the musketeers against cavalry or infantry charges while they reloaded.

The usual battlefield tactic was for the mixed groups of musketeers and halbardiers to form up in the centre with cavalry on the flanks. The infantry would advance to within musket range, then around 80

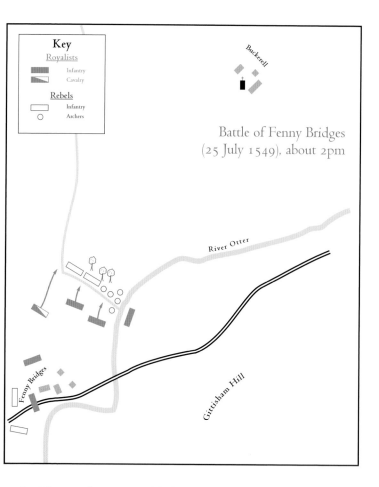

Key

Royalists

Infantry

Cavalry

Rebels

Infantry

Archers

Buckerell

Battle of Fenny Bridges
(25 July 1549), about 2pm

River Otter

Fenny Bridges

Gittisham Hill

yards. The musketeers would then open fire, reloading and firing
again and again until the enemy forces had been sufficiently depleted.
The halbardiers would then advance to engage in hand-to-hand
combat. Once the enemy had broken, the cavalry would be let loose
to pursue them off the field and prevent them from reforming.

Russell was a competent commander who understood the tactics of his day and well knew the potential of the various weaponry available to both sides. Having surveyed the positions taken up by the rebels, he set his own men in to battle order.

On his right flank he sent forward a mass of musketeers. They advanced down to the north of the road along the line of the modern railway. They halted on the bank of the Otter and opened fire on the rebel archers. Protected by the river these musketeers did not need halbardiers close by, so those units were added to the main column that was sent to assault the bridge. As Russell had planned the rebel archers concentrated on shooting at the musketeers so his assault column was able to reach the eastern end of the bridge in good order and full strength.

The fighting on and around the bridge was savage. Both sides were equipped with halbard and sword, so the cut and thrust was at very close quarters. Slowly the rebels fell back until the Royalists had established a secure area on the west bank of the river.

2. Recross the bridge and walk west about 150 yards to where a lane comes down from the north.

It was at about this spot that Russell unleashed his battle winning attack. Having pushed the rebels back from the bridge he had enough space on the west bank of the river to form up his troops. First to attack was a column of halbardiers who stormed forward in a dense formation that simply crashed through the weakened rebel lines. As they pushed forward, a body of cavalry trotted over the bridge to form up on the ground vacated by the halbardiers.

The right wing of the rebel army, including all the less well equipped men, was thrown into confusion by the attack of halbardiers and fell back down the road toward Exeter. They quickly lost formation and the retreat became a rout.

△ The lane to Buckerell twists and turns past farms and fields.

▷ Buckerell church has changed very little since the day of the battle.

From Buckerell the walk follows this lane downhill towards the Otter.

3. Turn right at the road junction and walk north, passing under first a railway bridge and then a second bridge that carries the A30 as it bypasses the village of Fenny Bridges. On the far side of the bridges the battle monument stands to the right of the road. The field behind the monument is where the Cornish archers stood. Emerging from under the two bridges, turn right into a narrow lane that then crosses a small stream.

The left flank of the rebel army was pushed along this route by the Royalist attack. The fields around the stream were occupied by the Cornish archers who were still engaged in their duel with the musketeers across the river. The archers now directed their shafts into the advancing Royalist halbardiers. The dense formation was an ideal target and despite their heavy armour the Royalists began to sustain losses. The retreating rebels rallied along the banks of the stream, their commanders pushing them into a new defensive formation.

Alerted to the trouble, Russell diverted his second body of cavalry away from the rout to the south and brought them up to this position. Reorganising his halbardiers and horsemen, Russell threw forward a new attack that crashed over the stream and smashed the reforming rebels. The fighting here was, if anything, even more prolonged than it had been at the bridge. So many corpses littered the ground that the local villagers dubbed the area 'Blood Meadow', a name it still retains.

4. Continue along lane through a small patch of woodland. The lane runs up the shallow valley of the stream, then bears right to reach the hamlet of Buckerell.

It was probably along roughly this route that the rebel left wing fled, pursued by Russell's cavalry. Some of the rebels fled to

Buckerell church to seek sanctuary, others ran up into the hills to the north. Russell was aware that he had defeated only a part of the rebel army. Impressive though the victory had been, it was far from decisive. The main rebel army lay ahead of him.

5. In Buckerell turn right, then right again to reach the church. After visiting the church, leave the churchyard by way of the lychgate and turn right into Cabbage Lane. At the end of this lane a track runs off to the left, heading south. At its end climb a stile into a field and cross this to reach the banks of the Otter. Cross the river by means of a footbridge and climb a slope to join the lane that was the main road from Honiton to Exeter before the A30 was built.

This was the road along which Russell and his army advanced to battle on the morning of 26 July.

6. Turn right and follow the lane down a gentle slope. Then turn sharp left to go under the A30 and the railway, then bear right and follow the road down to Fenny Bridges and the starting point of the walk.

△ The stout wooden bridge that carries the path from Buckerell over the Otter.

▷ The walk goes over this stile to join the road back down to Fenny Bridges.

8. CLYST ST MARY
1549

Distance:	5 miles.
Terrain:	Mostly over well-maintained footpaths or lanes. One lengthy section around the Grindle Brook is often muddy.
Public Transport:	Stagecoach bus route 52a runs to Clyst St Mary from Exeter.
Parking:	On-street parking available in the village.
Refreshments:	The walk passes three pubs serving meals.

After the defeat of their attempted pre-emptive strike at the Battle of Fenny Bridges, the rebels led by Sir Humphrey Arundel fell back on their camp outside the city of Exeter. They had lost about 500 men in the battle and the returning remnants of the defeated detachment rejoined their comrades who had been left to continue the blockade of the city. Despite the losses the rebels still had over 9,000 men in all.

Arundel must have guessed that he had little time to prepare for the Royalist onslaught, but in fact he had rather longer than he imagined. Although Lord Russell had convincingly defeated the rebel force at Fenny Bridges he was painfully aware that this had been only a part of their total force. He was still outnumbered by about 3:2 and the dogged resistance of the rebels convinced him that he would be hard pushed to defeat their main force in open battle. Accordingly he fell back to Honiton and sent Sir Peter Carew riding hard to London to ask for reinforcements.

Reaching London, Carew was ushered into the presence of the twelve-year-old King Edward VI, his regent the Duke of Somerset and the Royal Council. Carew made his report, then passed on Lord Russell's request for reinforcements. Somerset was in a delicate position at this moment. The new Prayer Book had largely been his work and was causing trouble not only in Devon but also in Wiltshire, Oxfordshire and East Anglia. The disturbances in

The church at Clyst St Mary was a focus for the rebels before the battle. The tower survives from the day of the battle, but most of the church is Victorian.

these areas were not so serious as in Devon, but the rioting and street fights were real enough to pose a threat to law and order.

Moreover his younger brother Thomas had recently been arrested on charges of treason for attempting to marry forcibly the Princess Elizabeth, then sixteen years old. Many suspected that Somerset had been involved in the plot to secure his family's grip on power should the increasingly frail King Edward die. Somerset was in no mood to hear that the rising in Devon was anything more than an easily dealt with local difficulty.

As Carew stopped speaking, Somerset turned on him. The Carews were a famously Catholic Cornish family and Somerset denounced Carew and his like as being behind the trouble in the first place. What followed was one of the most dramatic scenes in

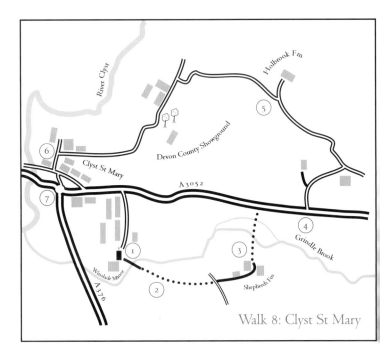

Walk 8: Clyst St Mary

Tudor history. Carew lost his temper, hurled accusations of maladministration and cowardice at Somerset, and ended up challenging him to a fight. The men were kept apart only by members of the Council who grabbed the hot-headed Cornishman and pushed him into his seat. In the tense silence that followed King Edward ordered that reinforcements be sent to Russell at Honiton. It was the beginning of the end for Somerset as regent and within a year he had been stripped of his offices.

Carew returned to Honiton in early August, bringing with him Lord Grey and 300 crack German mercenaries. A force of a thousand Welsh soldiers was also on the march and was expected to arrive within a week or two. Emboldened by the reinforcements,

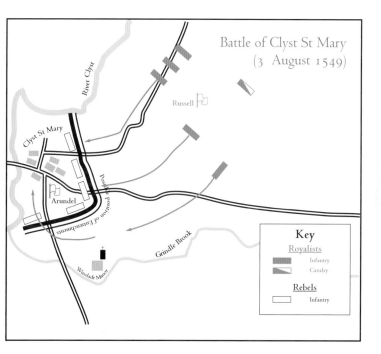

Battle of Clyst St Mary
(3 August 1549)

River Clyst

Russell

Clyst St Mary

Possible position of Entrenchments

Arundel

Grindle Brook

Winslade Manor

Key

Royalists

Infantry

Cavalry

Rebels

Infantry

Russell set off to raise the siege of Exeter and crush the rebels.

Russell's advance began well. As he pushed west from Honiton his scouts ranged widely, reporting back that the rebels had lifted the blockade of the city. Russell ordered a convoy of food wagons to head for the hungry city, then turned south toward the main rebel camp that was known to be at Clyst St Mary.

THE WALK

1. In Clyst St Mary find the parish church. To the north of the church Church Lane runs to the A3052.

△ The path away from the church is marked by this clear signage courtesy of Devon County Council.

◁ Beyond a small stream the walk passes through a little wood, then emerges into this open field. It leaves by means of a stile on the far side.

The rebels had taken over this church and made it their own. All traces of the Protestant faith were stripped from the church on the orders of Arundel and only the old rites permitted. The men of the army worshiped here daily, their own priest performing the rituals for the resident vicar had fled when the army first arrived. The church was substantially rebuilt in Victorian times, but the tower and nave are original.

In placing his camp, Arundel had positioned himself carefully. To the west was the River Clyst and to the south the broad, boggy Grindle Brook. The camp could be approached easily only from the north-east, and that area had been thoroughly prepared. During the long weeks that Exeter had been blockaded, Arundel had had his men hard at work with shovels digging entrenchments and field fortifications to block the access to Clyst St Mary.

Before the uprising had begun Arundel had been governor of the castle at St Michael's Mount. He had brought with him several light cannon. These were not powerful enough to make much impression on the walls of Exeter, but would be useful in an open fight. They were put under the control of a master gunner named John Hammond, who positioned them carefully among the field works being dug around the village.

The precise location and design of these defences has been lost over the years as the area has been redeveloped and built over. From some accounts it seems that the church was within the defended perimeter, though others indicate that it was outside. If it were in the defended area it is likely that the entrenchments ran north along roughly the line of Church Lane. Certainly the church tower was a key look out post from which rebel sentries kept a constant and vigilant watch for approaching enemies.

2. Turn right on leaving the church yard to walk along a track down to the Grindle Brook. Beyond the stream the track

becomes a footpath. Follow this path over open fields to reach a lane.

3. Cross the lane and walk up the track that leads to Shepherd's Farm. At the farmyard turn left and leave by way of a footpath that recrosses Grindle Brook, and a branch of it, to emerge on the main A3052.

4. Turn right along the A3052. After about 200 yards turn left into a narrow lane. At a Y-junction bear right, then turn left at a T-junction and follow the lane north-west to where a lane turns off sharp left.

It was at about this spot that Lord Russell, marching south along the east bank of the Clyst, first saw the rebel defences around Clyst St Mary. He will have paused here to survey the enemy preparations and formulate his plan for attack. The various reports of this battle give different dates for the main assault. It may be that Russell spent a day or two scouting out the defences before attacking. The most likely date for the battle is 3 August, but it may have taken place a day or two later.

As a defensive position the rebel base was, indeed, strong but it had its weaknesses. The key point from Russell's point of view was that the rebel camp lay on the east bank of the River Clyst. South of Clyst St Mary that river became increasingly wide, sluggish and marshy, making it difficult to cross. This is not so clear nowadays as the river has been channelled and the marshes drained but in 1549 it was a formidable obstacle. The only link between the rebels and their homes was a single bridge over the Clyst. If Russell could capture that bridge the rebels would be trapped.

Arundel had spotted the same fact. The key bridge was within the defensive perimeter and was guarded by the strongest earth-

◁ One of several stiles that carries the path between the church and Shepherd's Farm. The meadows can be very muddy in wet weather.

▽ Another of Devon Council's fine bridges carries the walk over the brook towards the A3052.

◁ The lane towards the County Showground. It was along this route that the Royalist army approached to do battle with the rebels in around Clyst St Mary.

▽ A roadside cottage beside the County Showground on the approaches to the village of Clyst St Mary.

works and by John Hammond with his cannon. Despite these obviously impressive obstacles, Russell decided to attack.

The route taken by the Royalist army as it marched to assault the rebel lines is now covered by the County Showground and cannot be accessed by the public. The walk now follows a route that takes it outside the right flank of the Royalist advance for a while.

5. Turn left at the lane as it skirts the northern edge of the County Showground. At a T-junction turn left. Follow this lane past the County Showground entrance. Pause where the lane swings to the left to head almost due west.

It was about here that the Royalist army assaulted the rebel defences, though the site can be placed only approximately. The fighting here was fierce for Arundel had put his best men to defend this vital spot.

In fact the rebel defences were first pierced on their southern edge, close to the church, by a secondary attack that had been intended as much as a diversion as anything else. The Royalist troops surged through the village centre, setting fire to the houses as they passed. Seeing the ominous columns of smoke rising into the sky, the rebels facing Russell's main assault lost heart and began to fall back over the bridge.

It was at this key moment that the gunner John Hammond was killed. As soon as he went down his gun crews abandoned their weapons and bolted for the bridge. The rest of the rebel army followed and the defeat became a rout.

6. Follow the lane to where it jinks sharp left beside a pub then reaches a T-junction. Turn right to find the Clyst St Mary bridge.

The bridge at Clyst St Mary is more of a causeway as it runs across the floodplain of the river. This proved to be a fatal bottleneck for the retreating rebels.

The bridge that stands here today is not the original, as it was rebuilt about 150 years after the battle. However it was reconstructed on the original piers and is probably about the same size and width as the one that was here in 1549. There were some 7,000 rebels clamouring to get over the bridge to escape the swords of the Royalists. The confusion was immense. Many men chose to swim the river instead. Hundreds of men were cut down trying to escape and many hundreds more were captured.

In all about a thousand rebels had been killed and another thousand captured, most of them injured. The battle had a nasty aftermath the following day. Lord Grey and his German mercenaries were escorting those prisoners able to walk back to Honiton when they came across a large band of rebels. Fearing he was about to be

The high street at Clyst St Mary was the scene of savage fighting as the rebel retreat became a rout.

attacked and that the prisoners might join their comrades, Grey ordered the German mercenaries to slit the throats of all the prisoners. As the massacre took place the band of rebels – in truth a leaderless mob of fugitives – fled.

As he left the field of battle Arundel must have known that his rebellion was as good as over, but he was not yet ready to give up. There was to be one more conflict before that would happen.

7. From the bridge return east, passing the lane by which you entered. Walk up the high street of the village, where fierce fighting raged as house-to-house struggles took place. Where the street meets the main road, turn left, then right down Church Lane to return to the church.

The church at Sampford Courtenay, where the Prayer Book Rebellion began with a protest about the vicar's robes.

9. SAMPFORD COURTNEY
1549

Distance:	2½ miles.
Terrain:	Mostly over well maintained lanes.
Public transport:	Stagecoach bus route 51 runs to Sampford Courtney from Exeter.
Parking:	On-street parking available in the village.
Refreshments:	One pub serving meals and bar snacks.

The Prayer Book Rebellion of 1549 that led to the battles at Fenny Bridges and Clyst St Mary had been sparked by an uproar in the parish church at Sampford Courtenay, so it was apt that the rebellion should come to a bloody conclusion in this same village.

The uprising takes its name from the fact that it was the forcible imposition of a standard and strictly Protestant service book on the church in England that both sparked the trouble and which was used as a rallying cry by the Catholic gentry who led the movement. In fact many of the men who joined the uprising were motivated as much by anger at the enclosure of open land and the severe economic crisis as by religious motives.

After the defeat at Clyst St Mary most of the rebels took the opportunity to slip off home. The rebellion was clearly doomed and the Royalist commanders had shown themselves to be in vengeful mood. By 10 August, when Sir Humphrey Arundel mustered the remaining rebels at Sampford Courtenay, only those motivated primarily by religion and unwilling to compromise were left. He had perhaps 2,000 men with him.

Arundel would have known that execution was the only fate that awaited him and his fellow rebel leaders. While the government had been fairly lenient in dealing with outbreaks of unrest elsewhere in England, there was every indication that the religious motivation of the rebels in Devon would mean they would be treated severely. Those at Sampford Courtenay probably expected to die one way or another.

Arundel set his men to work to fortify the village for a last stand. Coming against him was a royal army made up of around 3,000 Englishmen under Lord Russell, some 300 German mercenaries led by Lord Grey and about 1,000 Welsh professionals commanded by Sir William Herbert.

THE WALK

1. In Sampford Courtenay find the church.

It was in this church that the parishioners of the village had on Whit Monday forced their preacher to use the old rites of the Catholic church that had been banned by the new Prayer Book. The church contains impressive information boards, memorials and other information about the Prayer Book Rebellion. It well repays a visit, and makes a contribution to the church fund worthwhile.

The uproar led to a riot in which a local farmer, who rode into the village to calm things down, was killed. Most of the villagers promptly fled home, but the more militant armed themselves and marched on Exeter. As they went the protesters gathered supporters from the villages they passed. They hoped to confront the Bishop of Exeter and argue the case for tolerance of different church rituals, but were met by the locked gates of Exeter. While they were camped outside Exeter waiting to meet the bishop they were met by Sir Humphrey Arundel and his armed men. Thus was the rebellion begun.

◁ The village sign for Sampford Courtenay keeps memoris of the Prayer Book Rebellion alive into the twenty-first century.

▽ The death of William Hellyons, the first of about 5,000 men to die in the Prayer Book Rebellion, is commemorated by this plaque in the village high street.

On Whit Monday 1549
SAMPFORD COURTENAY
people killed a local farmer
WILLIAM HELLYONS
and then joined the Cornish in
the Prayer Book Rebellion which
ended in defeat by the King's army
outside this village

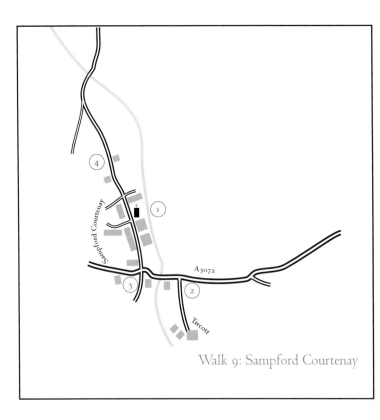

Walk 9: Sampford Courtenay

2. Leave the church by way of the lychgate and turn left down the village high street. At the junction with Green Hill turn left to join the A3072. Follow the road for about 300 yards to lane on the right leading to Trecott.

It was along this route that the protesters had left the village on their way to Exeter, and along this road that the remnant of the rebel army trailed into the village some months later. The hill to the north of the A3072, Green Hill was the scene of the main rebel camp.

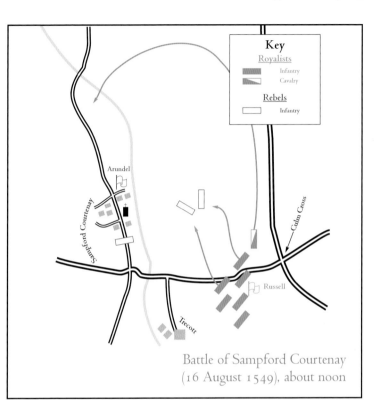

Battle of Sampford Courtenay
(16 August 1549), about noon

Around mid-morning on 16 August, the tell-tale plume of dust was seen rising into the summer air. The enemy was approaching. The scouts rode back to Sampford Courtenay to inform their comrades that battle was imminent.

As soon as the rebel lookout had gone Royalist scouts came spurring up the hill from the Taw to occupy Culm Cross. From there they pushed cautiously along the road toward Sampford Courtenay. They did not need to go far before they saw the earthwork and timber fortifications that the rebels had been constructing.

Green Hill, east of the village centre, was the site of the main rebel camp before the battle.

The village high street. Few of the houses that stand here today existed on the day of the battle, most of them dating to a century of more later, but the layout remains the same.

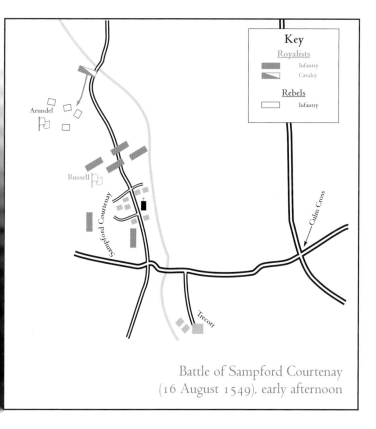

Battle of Sampford Courtenay
(16 August 1549), early afternoon

The works on top of Green Hill were not completed by the time the Royalists attacked. After some fighting the rebels fell back to the more easily defended village, the houses of which had been barricaded and fortified. Lord Russell had overcome more impressive defences at Clyst St Mary just over a week earlier, so he must have deployed his men to take these with some confidence.

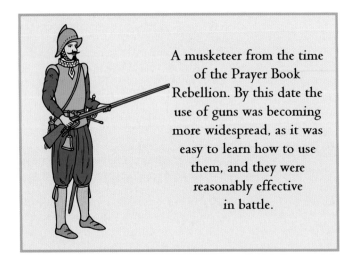

A musketeer from the time of the Prayer Book Rebellion. By this date the use of guns was becoming more widespread, as it was easy to learn how to use them, and they were reasonably effective in battle.

3. Return back along the main road, turning right to enter the high street. Walk north past the church and out of the village along the lane to Honeychurch to reach a junction with a lane coming from the left.

On the day of battle the village began about 150 yards up this lane. The main defensive works were located very close to the first cottages, so they would have stood across this lane and in what are now the gardens of the more modern houses. Russell sent his German mercenaries and English infantry into the assault. Firing muskets at close quarters, then charging home with halbards and swords the attackers made short work of any resistance. Within minutes the Royalists were clambering over the scant fortifications and smashing their way into the houses using axes and gunbutts.

There was a rally by Arundel and his men outside the church, but the Royalists were charging up the street in numbers. The rebels

Although muskets had a range of around 100 yards by the 1540s, they were prone to misfire and slow to load. Groups of musketeers were accompanied into battle by halbardiers, whose swords and axe-headed halberds were not so prone to fail in battle.

did not stand for long before their formation broke and they began streaming north up the lane towards the village of Honeychurch.

Somewhere along this route, the fleeing rebels ran headlong into a trap set by Lord Russell. Before ordering the assault on the village and its defences he had sent the Royalist cavalry riding down the east bank of the stream to cross half a mile or more below the village. It was about here that they were launched in a terrifying charge at the enemy. The rebels were disordered and already in retreat. They were in no condition to withstand a cavalry charge. The rout was turned in minutes into a massacre.

The rebels broke completely and fled in all directions, harried and pursued by the flickering swords of the Royalist cavalry. The chase and the killing lasted for the rest of the day. By dusk some 700 rebels had been killed and another 700 captured, the rest having escaped.

4. Return to the church where the walk started.

It was here that Lord Russell set his camp the night after the battle. Arundel was dragged in front of him and put in chains, as were other leaders of the rebellion. A day or two later Russell left for London taking with him the rebel leaders, the German mercenaries and his English troops. Arundel and his fellow rebels were later tried in London, convicted of treason and executed.

In Devon and Cornwall, meanwhile, Sir Anthony Kingstone had been given the task of tracking down any rebels that had escaped and had the 1,000 Welshmen to enforce his orders. Kingstone was a Protestant of the most fanatical kind. He used his men to break into houses looking for any signs of Catholicism. If a crucifix or other suspect object was found the men were free to plunder the house, beating up or killing anyone who objected.

When Kingstone reached Bodmin, a town from which several men had gone to join the uprising, he ordered a gallows to be built in the market place while his men ransacked the houses in search of rebels. That evening Kingstone dined at the town hall with the mayor of Bodmin. As the meal finished Kingstone turned to the mayor and asked 'Do you think my men have made a fine job of that gibbet?'

The mayor eyed the construction nervously being all too aware of the help he had given the protesters before the movement had become a fully fledged rebellion. 'Aye,' he replied. 'It seems stout enough.'

'Well then,' glowered Kingstone summoning three of his men. 'You had better go up there and test it.' Such brutal behaviour earned Kingstone an evil reputation. It is thought that he and his men killed over 500 men in the weeks that followed the Battle at Sampford Courtenay.

△ The rebels sought to make a final stand here, where the high street opens out in front of the church, but they failed to stem the Royalist advance.

▷ The aftermath of the Prayer Book Rebellion can be clearly seen inside the village church. The north wall contains this door that is reached by means of a spiral staircase from the opening on the right. The door originally gave access to the top of the rood screen that separated the nave from the chancel. The sweeping away of such a physical barrier between congregation and clergy was a key aim of the Protestant reformers against which the rebellion was organized.

10. MODBURY
1642 & 1643

Distance:	3½ miles.
Terrain:	Mostly over surfaced lanes; however, one section is over open fields. There are two steepish, but short hills on the walk.
Public transport:	First Bus route 93 runs to Modbury from Plymouth.
Parking:	Limited on-street parking in the village.
Refreshments:	Two pubs serving meals in the village as well as a small grocers selling snacks.

The causes of the English Civil War of the mid-seventeenth century were complex. Some felt that political considerations were the more important, either wanting to advance the power of Parliament or to enforce the rights of the King. Others saw religion as more important with Protestants backing the radicals in Parliament and the moderates favouring the King's support for the established Church of England. Still others were more concerned with ridding England of the inept ministers that King Charles had chosen. For many it was a mix of motives that led them to chose the side they did.

Whatever the motivations that led England into civil war, the south-west of England was generally for the king when Charles I raised the Royal Standard in August 1642 and summoned all loyal Englishmen to join his army. A striking exception was the city and port of Plymouth, which declared for Parliament and closed its gates to the county authorities who supported the king.

At first few men took the prospect of civil war seriously. Several weeks passed without serious fighting as both sides sought to take control of armouries, fortresses and civic treasuries. Both King and Parliament thought the other would back down rather than force a conflict. It was not until after the first large scale battle at Edgehill

◁ Modbury's war memorial commemorates conflicts of the twentieth century, but makes a convenient starting point from which to explore the town's role in those of the seventeenth century.

▽ The view down into Modbury that would have greeted the Roundhead troopers as they launched their dawn attack on 7 December 1642. The assault achieved a complete surprise.

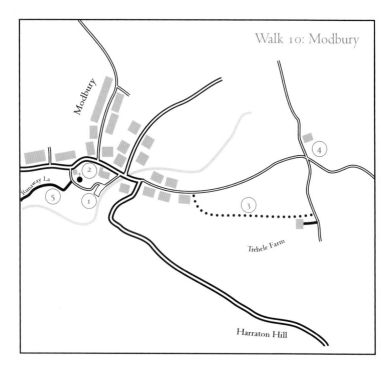

Walk 10: Modbury

in October that it dawned on most men that the war was to be taken seriously.

Sir Ralph Hopton, a gentleman from Somerset, was appointed the king's commander in the south-west. He ordered the loyal men of South Devon to muster for war at the church at Modbury on 6 December 1642. Each man was to bring with him whatever he had in the way of weapons. Hopton planned to organise the men in to regiments once they had arrived. Those with good weapons were to be fighting troops, those without to form supply units or train as siege engineers or to be used for the manual labour that all armies need.

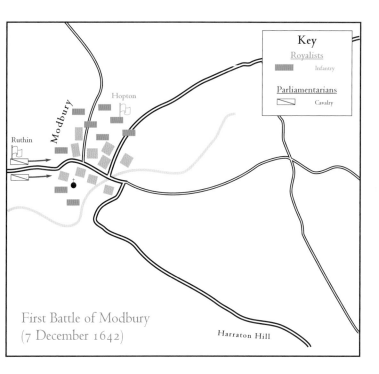

First Battle of Modbury
(7 December 1642)

When Hopton arrived he was pleased to find that more than 3,000 men had turned up. The task of getting them organised into an army would begin the next day. Unfortunately for Hopton the Parliamentarian garrison of Plymouth had heard of the muster and were determined to intervene.

THE WALK

1. In Modbury walk west up the hill and along the A379 to find the war memorial on the left near the top of the hill.

It was down this road at dawn on 7 December that a force of 500 Roundhead troopers came galloping at full speed led by Colonel Ruthin. The professional horsemen wasted little time, but at once went to work attacking the sleepy Royalists as they stumbled from their beds and tents. Hopton himself narrowly escaped a sweeping sword blade before he managed to get on horseback and try to organise a rally, but it was too late. The Roundheads swept through the town with ruthless efficiency and the forming Royalist army was scattered across the fields of south Devon. This First Battle of Modbury was over quickly and few men lost their lives – neither would be true of the Second Battle of Modbury.

2. Return to the village centre to find the Exeter Arms Hotel on the left.

The skirmish of December proved to be only a temporary setback for the king's cause in Devon. Hopton was an energetic and skilled soldier who quickly overcame his difficulties to build up a sizeable army which he was determined to get trained to a semblance of professional efficiency before leading it into battle. By January he had established a secure land blockade around Plymouth. Although the Parliamentary garrison could bring in supplies and reinforcements by sea, the normal life of the city was to be slowly strangled by the blocking of all roads in and out of the countryside surrounding Plymouth.

Modbury was in a key strategic position as it commanded the narrow gap between the heights of Dartmoor and the sea a few miles east of Plymouth. Hopton stationed Sir Nicholas Slanning and Colonel Trevanion in the town with about 2,000 men. The senior officers lodged in the Exeter Arms Hotel. Their orders were to patrol the roads leading to Plymouth. Everyone using the roads was to be stopped and searched, with anyone suspicious being

The Exeter Inn was where some of the Royalist officers were staying when the Roundheads attacked on 7 December. The Cavaliers manged to get out after a brief scuffle, but were unable to rally their men to face the surprise attack.

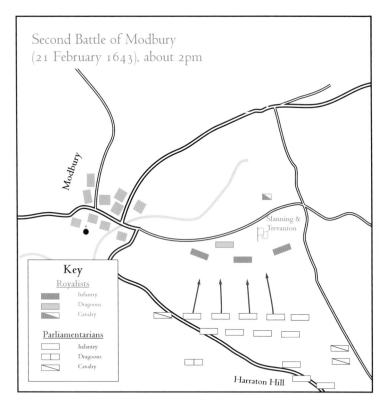

Second Battle of Modbury
(21 February 1643), about 2pm

Modbury

Slanning &
Trevanion

Key

Royalists

Infantry

Dragoons

Cavalry

Parliamentarians

Infantry

Dragoons

Cavalry

Harraton Hill

arrested and taken away for questioning. Slanning and Trevanion did their job well and the eastern roads into Plymouth were securely blocked.

The winter of 1642–3 was exceptionally mild, which allowed armies to operate when they would normally be shivering in winter quarters. On 19 January Hopton's main army of 8,000 men defeated some 5,000 Parliamentarians under Colonel Ruthin. Ruthin and his men had been trying to reach Launceston, but were stopped at Braddock Down and rolled back to Liskeard.

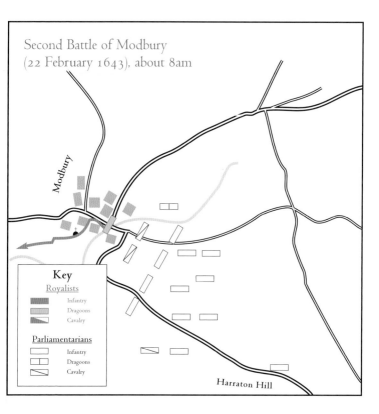

Second Battle of Modbury
(22 February 1643), about 8am

Modbury

Key

Royalists

Infantry
Dragoons
Cavalry

Parliamentarians

Infantry
Dragoons
Cavalry

Harraton Hill

Meanwhile a second Roundhead army was on the march, and this time it had not been spotted by Hopton's scouts. This army was some 8,000 strong and was marching down from Bristol with the aim of breaking through to Plymouth and raising the blockade of that city. On 19 February the army marched into Totnes unopposed for there were no Royalist troops present. They strode out at dawn and that evening camped at Kingsbridge. A local man managed to get away on horseback, riding hard for Modbury to alert Slanning and Trevanion to the approaching danger.

Early on the morning of 21 February Slanning and Trevanion mustered their men in the little village square. They had some 1,500 men with them, the rest being off on patrol. Messengers were sent out to gather the scattered units and bring them back to Modbury, but that would take time. Even if all the patrols came in the Royalists would still be outnumbered by 4:1. A rider was sent off to find Hopton and give him the news.

After giving their men a good breakfast to sustain them through the coming day Slanning and Trevanion led them out to take up a defensive position east of the village.

3. Head east along the A379. Where the main road turns sharp right go straight on into Galpin Street. Follow this steep lane up and out of the village. Just past the last house on the right a footpath leaves the lane by way of a flight of steps and a stile. It then strikes off across the open hillside, crossing several fields and stiles as it does so. After about 150 yards the path tops the crest of the hill.

It was on this hilltop that the Royalists formed up to face the coming onslaught. In 1643 this whole area was divided up into a mass of small fields, each bordered by dense hedgerows that formed impressive obstacles to fighting men. Slanning and Trevanion positioned their men carefully among these natural barricades, some of which remain. They had five pieces of light artillery that were placed so as to have sweeping arcs of fire down the southern face of the hill up which the Parliamentarians would need to attack.

The vast majority of the Royalist troops were infantry, and there were no real cavalry. Slanning and Trevanion did have about 500 dragoons.

By this date infantry tactics were a refined development of those that had prevailed among the government troops during the Prayer

◁ The flight of steps set into a stone wall that carries the walk up out of town and into the open fields where most of the fighting took place during the Second Battle of Modbury.

▽ The view from the right flank of the initial Royalist position, looking south-east. The Roundhead army came marching over the hill, heading towards Plymouth.

One of the banked hedges that criss-cross the hill east of Modbury. These naturally strong obstacles stand around 5 feet tall. The Royalists had spent some hours fortifying these banked hedges before the battle, turning each into a miniature redoubt.

Book Rebellion a century earlier. There were two main types of infantry: musketeers and pikemen. The musketeers were armed with muskets that by this date were reasonably reliable in battle. They could send a lead ball a distance of abut 150 yards, though were accurate at only about 75 yards. Trained men could fire once every 45 seconds or so, though once a minute was more usual. Musketeers formed up in dense ranks so that their inaccurate weapons could be discharged in massed volleys that stood a chance of hitting the enemy.

The halbardiers had been replaced by pikemen equipped with pikes up to 16 feet long and wearing heavier armour. These men guarded the musketeers against a sudden charge by cavalry or infantry while they were reloading, and could be used to assault

△ One of the old-style stone stiles over which the walk crosses on its way to the battlefield.

▷ On the far side of the battlefield the walks goes through this metal gate to enter a lane beside a farm.

enemy formations with 'push of pike' when they would advance forward at a walk with pikes levelled at chest height.

Cavalry were used principally for scouting and pursuit, though there was a growing tendency for them to be used on the battlefield to charge enemy formations to break them up. Dragoons were primarily lightly armed infantry who rode around the battlefield, but dismounted to fight. They were useful for lightning strikes and fast-moving raids but lacked the armour and staying power of the true infantry.

The composition of the advancing Parliamentarian army has not been recorded, but it seems to have been mostly composed of infantry with about a thousand cavalry but few, if any, dragoons.

It was an hour after noon when the waiting Cavaliers saw the enemy advancing up the road from Kingsbridge. As they came over the shoulder of Harraton Hill, the Parliamentarians turned off the road to form up for the attack. The first attack went in at about 2 o'clock. The Parliamentarian infantry came marching up the slope in massed columns, but the Royalist musketeers opened fire from behind their hedges with skill and determination. The Parliamentarians came on steadily and the battle soon became a confused series of small fights for the control of hedges and ditches.

Dusk in February comes early and by the time the light was fading the Royalists still held the crest of this hill. As dark night settled over the battlefield, the Parliamentarians called off their attacks and fell back down the hill. Slanning and Trevanion had done well to hold their own in the face of overwhelming odds, but they were under no illusions. The next day would bring fresh attacks and they could not hope to hold out for a full day of fighting.

A force of some 300 dragoons was positioned on and around the hilltop. Their orders were to keep on the move throughout the night, firing volleys of musketry from different positions toward the enemy at odd intervals throughout the night. Come dawn they were to retreat.

Meanwhile, Slanning and Trevanion mustered their infantry as quietly as possible in the dark and led them off.

4. Continue along the path along the slope over which the fighting had raged until it meets a lane. Turn left and at a crossroads turn left again. This lane takes you back to Galpin Street. This time turn left down the lane to the car park. Just before the car park, bear right and climb up a narrow lane to reach the rear of the church.

This was the route taken by the retreating Royalist infantry as they slipped away in the night. Next dawn the Royalist dragoons

◁ After the battle proper, the retreating Royalist dragoons were caught by the Roundhead troopers as they tried to escape down this track, later dubbed Runaway Lane, beyond the church.

A bench sits beside the cobbled path that gives pedestrians safe passage around a blind corner on the lane that leads up to the church from the car park.

Modbury church stands atop the hill at the west end of town. It is little altered since the day of the battle, except for some damage that is usually ascribed to Roundhead troopers.

also came this way. After firing a final volley of musketry and blasting the Parliamentarians with a salvo from the cannon they leapt to their horses and fell back. But they had left it too late. The Parliamentarian cavalry had better mounts than the dragoons and gave swift chase.

It was around the churchyard that the Roundhead troopers caught up with the dragoons. A running fight developed as the horsemen raced down the track now known as Runaway Lane. About 30 Royalist dragoons were killed and 80 captured in the pursuit that went on for miles.

5. After exploring Runaway Lane on the left, just beyond the church, return and enter the churchyard by way of the gate. After exploring the church continue through the churchyard to reach the war memorial where the walk began.

It is worth exploring the church. After the battle the Roundheads stabled their horses in this church, causing a degree of damage to the interior monuments that can still be seen today.

The Parliamentarian infantry found in the town a store of over 1,000 muskets and almost as many pikes. In all the Royalists had lost about 100 killed and some 200 wounded, only some of whom had been taken away. Parliamentarian losses are not recorded, but must have been much the same.

The Royalists fell back to Plympton where they met Hopton marching up fast with a detachment. Once Hopton realised the size of the advancing army he ordered a retreat, lifting the siege of Plymouth. It proved to be only a temporary respite. When the Roundhead army returned to Bristol on other business, Hopton moved back to blockade Plymouth once again.

11. CHAGFORD
1643

Distance:	1¼ miles.
Terrain:	Surfaced paths within the village only.
Public transport:	Stagecoach bus route 173 to Chagford from Exeter.
Parking:	Car park in the village square.
Refreshments:	Several pubs serving meals and a shop selling snacks.

The early months of the English Civil War were spent by both sides seeking to enforce their grip on the local administrations of the country. Control of a local council meant that taxation from that town or county flowed to whichever side had secured control, and if a town or city had an armoury then those weapons were at the disposal of whoever secured it first.

While most of Devon declared for the King, some of the small industrial towns preferred the Parliamentarian cause. Chagford was one such and in February a small troop of Parliamentarian horse was sent to the town to secure it against the Royalist forces mustering in Devon. Colonel Northcote and his officers stayed at Whyddon House, now the Three Crowns Hotel, while the men were billeted in the houses of the town.

The Royalists were, indeed, in the process of occupying all of Devon. Chagford was known to be hostile to their cause, but that made their commander, Sir Ralph Hopton, all the more determined to capture it and ensure that taxes due to the government from the town went to the King, not to Parliament. When he heard that Northcote and his men had arrived in the town, Hopton sent his own Colonel Berkeley with a troop of cavalry, and another of dragoons, to attack.

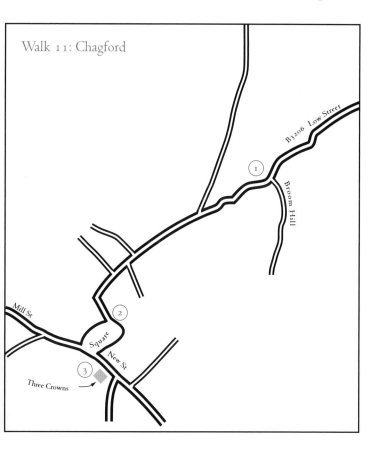

THE WALK

1. In Chagford walk out along the B3206 Low Street to the junction with Broom Hill on the right.

The Cavalier cavalry came clattering down this lane at dawn on 8 February 1643. A Parliamentarian picket was posted somewhere

The view towards Chagford from the approach lane. The Royalist horse came trotting up this lane at dawn to launch a surprise attack on a body of Roundheads that had taken up quarters in the little town.

about here. He heard the horsemen approaching and raced back to Chagford to alert his comrades. The Roundheads seem to have reacted quickly for they were tumbling out of their cottages, swords and pistols in hand as the Cavaliers burst in amongst them.

2. Walk south-west along Low Street into the village centre and find the main square.

It was in this square that the main fighting took place. Being fully awake and mounted the Royalists had the advantage over the still sleepy Parliamentarians. A savage street fight erupted here, but the Cavaliers had a firm goal in mind.

3. From the square walk south-east into New Street to find the Three Crowns Inn on the right.

△ The narrow lane that gives access to the Market Square. The alarm had already been given by Roundhead sentries by the time the Cavaliers reached this point, but the attackers did not pause as they swept on towards their key objective.

▷ The market place is today dominated by this small council building, but at the time of the battle was an open area for stalls and merchants.

Led by the dashing Sir Sydney Godolphin, MP for Helston and famed poet, one squad of Cavaliers made straight for Whyddon House to tackle the Roundhead commanders. Northcote and his officers were by this time emerging from the house and a brisk fight erupted around the stone porch of the building. Godolphin received a pistol bullet in his thigh that severed a main artery and he collapsed to lean against the stone walls of the porch. His men redoubled their efforts and managed to get into the house, though Northcote escaped by scrambling out the back.

Most of the Roundhead troopers managed to get away, scattering across the hills to the south before reforming and heading east to more friendly territory. Chagford was secured for the King, though its citizens were none too pleased by the fact. The unfortunate Godolphin, however, was dying. He was carried into Whyddon House and made as comfortable as possible. His body was later taken to Okehampton for burial.

His death was much mourned in the West Country and local poet Clinton Scollard later penned the lines:

> They rode from the camp at morn
> With clash of sword and spur.
> The birds were loud in the thorn,
> The sky was an azure blur.
> A gallant show they made
> That warm noontide of the year,
> Led on by a dashing blade,
> By the poet-cavalier.
>
> They laughed through the leafy lanes,
> The long lanes of Dartmoor;
> And they sang their soldier strains,
> Pledged 'death' to the Roundhead boor;

▷ The entrance porch of the Three Crowns at Chagford. The Roundhead officers were staying here and a fierce struggle around the entrance took place as the Cavaliers sought to break in.

▽ The view from Chagford churchyard toward the distant moors.

Then they came at the middle day
To a hamlet quaint and brown
Where the hated troopers lay,
And they cheered for the King and crown.

They fought in the fervid heat,
Fought fearlessly and well,
But low at the foeman's feet
Their valorous leader fell.
Full on his fair young face
The blinding sun beat down;
In the morn of his manly grace
He died for the King and crown.

Oh the pitiless blow,
The vengeance-thrust of strife,
That blotted the golden glow
From the sky of his glad, brave life!
The glorious promise gone; –
Night with its grim black frown!
Never again the dawn,
And all for the King and crown.

Hidden his sad fate now
In the sealed book of the years;
Few are the heads that bow,
Or the eyes that brim with tears,
Reading 'twixt blots and stains
From a musty tome that saith
How he rode through the Dartmoor lanes
To his woeful, dauntless death.

But I, in the summer's prime,
From that lovely leafy land
Look back to the olden time
And the leal and loyal band.
I see them dash along, –
I hear them charge and cheer,
And my heart goes out in a song
To the poet-cavalier.

Chagford church has scarcely changed since the day of the skirmish. It is well worth a visit as it is one of the finest churches on the edge of Dartmoor.

12. SOURTON DOWN
1643

Distance:	1 mile.
Terrain:	Mostly over surfaced paths.
Public transport:	First Bus route 86 to Sourton Down from Okehampton.
Parking:	Car park off the A386 where the walk starts and finishes.
Refreshments:	The walk passes a restaurant and hotel where meals and bar snacks are served.

By the spring of 1643 the two sides in England's Civil War had each secured for themselves a part of the kingdom, money and men. It was clearly going to be a bloody and protracted war. King Charles decided that his most immediate aim should be to establish secure links between those parts of the country that had declared themselves loyal to himself. To this end Sir Ralph Hopton in command of the Royalist forces in the south-west was ordered to march

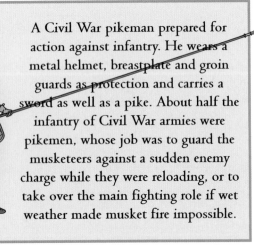

A Civil War pikeman prepared for action against infantry. He wears a metal helmet, breastplate and groin guards as protection and carries a sword as well as a pike. About half the infantry of Civil War armies were pikemen, whose job was to guard the musketeers against a sudden enemy charge while they were reloading, or to take over the main fighting role if wet weather made musket fire impossible.

towards Bristol, then held by Parliament, to capture the city and so establish a link to the Royalist areas of Wales and the Marches.

Although Parliament had little support in the south-west, they did hold the key towns and Hopton was understandably reluctant to march out of his home area leaving active enemy forces in his rear. Having first made sure that all enemy strongholds were securely invested by local forces, Hopton moved against the main Parliamentarian army in the south-west, 2,500 men under Colonel James Chudleigh. The two armies met outside Launceston and Hopton won a convincing victory that sent Chudleigh and his men retreating east to Okehampton.

Hopton was, for once, badly served by his scouts who assured him on the morning of 25 April 1643 that Chudleigh was continuing to retreat back towards Bristol. In fact he had halted in Okehampton having learned that the Earl of Stamford was coming to support him with an army of 3,000 men.

At noon the Royalists paused to eat lunch near Rexon, then pushed on. Hopton was hoping to reach Okehampton, which he

A Civil War musketeer. His musket is a heavy and cumbersome weapon that needs to be rested on the upright pole before it can be levelled and fired. He carries a number of pre-packed cartridges dangling from the baldric belt over his shoulder. The sword is for use at close quarters or in wet weather.

fondly believed to be deserted by the enemy, by nightfall. He was, as a result, moving more quickly than was wise in the presence of the enemy. By early evening the Royalist vanguard, made up of a regiment of Cornish infantry, had marched over Prewley Moor and was approaching Sourton Down. The wind was getting up and storm clouds hung low over Dartmoor to the south.

Chudleigh, for his part, knew exactly where Hopton and his men were. He ordered his infantry to draw up just south-west of Okehampton, then led his cavalry and dragoons toward Hopton, looking for a site suitable to lay an ambush. He chose South Down, the highest hill of Sourton Down. He was unwilling to risk his entire force in combat so soon after his defeat at Launceston and so left his infantry where they were to await his orders to advance or retreat depending on what happened.

THE WALK

1. It is unfortunate that in the years since the battle this strip of land just north of Dartmoor became one of the busiest through routes in Devon. First the London and Southwest Railway built a line through the centre of the battlefield in the mid-ninteenth century, then in the mid-twentieth century the government constructed the A30 dual carriageway trunk road alongside the railway. As a result of these changes it is possible to trace only a part of the battle on the ground. Find the car park that lies off the A386 immediately north of that road's junction with the A30.

The Cornish Royalists were advancing up what was then the Launceston Road, but which is now an unnumbered road running roughly parallel to and south of the A30. That road met the Tavistock Road, now the A386 at this spot. To the south, beyond the thundering

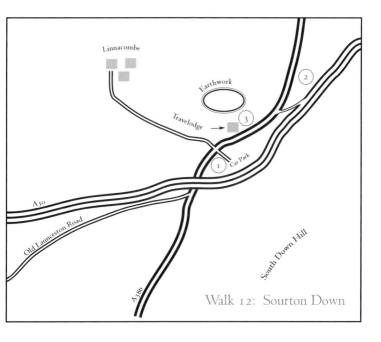

Walk 12: Sourton Down

traffic of the A30 rise the slopes of South Down. It was on these slopes, hiding behind some hedges, that Chudleigh and his men waited.

As the leading Cornishmen passed this spot, Chudleigh launched his attack. The horsemen came thundering down the slope, crossing what is now the disused railway and the busy A30. At the last moment the dragoons halted, leapt from their horses and fired a crushing volley into the surprised infantry. The cavalry came on, charging home and scattering the Royalists.

Surveying the scene of his success, Chudleigh sent a rider back to Okehampton ordering his infantry to hurry up to join him and exploit the victory. At this point the heavens opened and a torrential thunderstorm swept down over the scene. In the pouring rain Chudleigh rallied his horsemen and drew his now dismounted

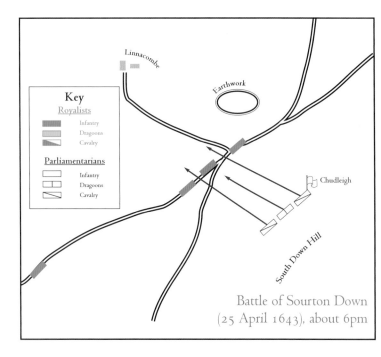

Battle of Sourton Down
(25 April 1643), about 6pm

dragoons up into a defensive formation blocking the main road.

Hopton, meanwhile, was also manoeuvring his men in the rain.
While his shaken Cornishmen rallied and reformed, Hopton got
his main body off the road and into a battle formation before
advancing cautiously back to Sourton Down. At this point he had
no idea exactly how many men Chudleigh had with him on the
field of battle.

As the Royalist army came up the slope they emerged across the
land where the A386 now passes under the A30. From here they
could see Chudleigh's men and Hopton realised that he was faced
by only a small force. He ordered an instant attack. The Royalist
advance pushed Chudleigh back with ease.

The site of the initial Parliamentarian attack on the advancing Royalists is now covered over by the A30 dual carriageway. This photo was taken from the position of the head of the Royalist column looking towards the direction from which the attack came.

The site of the main struggle at the start of the battle is now occupied by this Little Chef restaurant, a petrol station to the left and a hotel to the right.

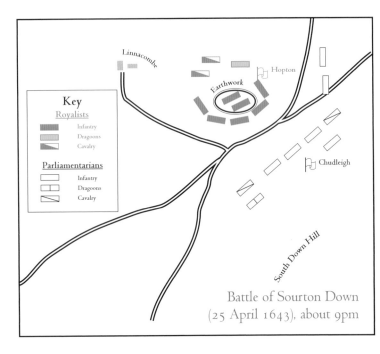

Linnacombe

Earthwork

Hopton

Chudleigh

Key

<u>Royalists</u>

Infantry

Dragoons

Cavalry

<u>Parliamentarians</u>

Infantry

Dragoons

Cavalry

South Down Hill

Battle of Sourton Down
(25 April 1643), about 9pm

2. Walk east along the A386 passing the petrol station, restaurant and Travelodge Hotel on your left. Continue to where a spur leads from The A386 to the eastbound carriageway of the A30.

When Hopton's men reached this point, they saw through the rain and gathering dusk the advancing columns of the Roundhead infantry marching west from Okehampton. In the appalling light Hopton could not make out how many men were advancing, but he reasoned that after his defeat Chudleigh would not be risking a major battle unless he had been reinforced. Thinking he was outnumbered, Hopton ordered his men to pull back to a prehistoric earthwork that lay off the road to the north.

3. Return to the petrol station and look into the field behind, where the humps and ditches of what remains of this earth-work can be seen.

It was completely dark by the time Chudleigh's infantry came up to the earthwork and the rain had not stopped. While Chudleigh weighed up his options, Hopton's artillery suddenly opened fire with devastating effect. Another salvo crashed out before the Parliamentarians realised that the Royalist gunners were firing at the dull red glows caused by the fuses attached to the musketeers weapons. The Roundheads began extinguishing the fuses, but Chudleigh hurriedly ordered them to stop. Instead he ordered them to drape the fuses over the gorse bushes that dotted Sourton Down.

Chudleigh then led his men back to Okehampton for a hot meal and a good night's rest. Back on Sourton Down, Hopton saw the glowing fuses and believed that the Roundheads were still present. Firing the occasional volley of musketry at the supposed foe, the Royalists spent a wet and uncomfortable night wide awake on the windswept hills. Some time before dawn, Hopton realised his mistake, but also recognised that his exhausted men were in no condition to fight a battle should Chudleigh reappear. He ordered a retreat to Launceston to recover.

4. Return to the car park and the start of the walk.

In fact Chudleigh waited until Stanford arrived before chasing Hopton's men into Cornwall. The armies met at Stratton, where Hopton won a convincing victory. Cornwall and Devon were thus secured for the King, with only Plymouth holding out.

13. TIVERTON
1645

Distance:	½ mile.
Terrain:	Entirely over surfaced footpaths.
Public transport:	Stagecoach bus route 55 runs to Tiverton from Exeter.
Parking:	Several car parks in the town.
Refreshments:	Several pubs in the town as well as shops selling snacks and soft drinks.

After his setback at Sourton Down, Sir Ralph Hopton won a stunning victory for the king in Cornwall at Stratton. Thereafter, apart from Plymouth, Devon was free of Parliamentarian soldiers for two years. By 1645, however, King Charles I had been doing badly throughout the rest of England. In September the key port of Bristol surrendered to Parliament. With Bristol captured and the king's army routed at Naseby, Parliament felt able to send forces into Devon once again. They put in command of the campaign their most feared commanders, Lord Fairfax and Oliver Cromwell.

On 17 October the columns of Fairfax's army were seen approaching Tiverton. The Royalist garrison abandoned the town as being too weak to be defended and retired into the castle. Fairfax and his men entered the town, took up lodgings and at once began to reconnoitre the castle and its defences. The castle of Tiverton had been built in 1106 and although it had been regularly updated since, it was far from being a modern or a powerful fortress. By 1645 modern artillery was able to smash even the stoutest stone walls given enough time and ammunition. All the garrison could hope to do was hold out until either help came or the Parliamentarians gave up and left. Neither was very likely.

△ The church at Tiverton was inside the Royalist defensive perimeter during the siege and received hits from several cannon balls. One side chapel was totally destroyed and the main building had to be repaired after the Roundheads left.

▷ The main gatehouse to Tiverton Castle. At the time of the siege this was fronted by a moat and drawbridge. It was the unexpected collapse of the drawbridge that ended the siege.

TIVERTON CASTLE

OPEN EASTER TO LATE JUNE
AND SEPTEMBER
SUNDAYS AND THURSDAYS
JULY AND AUGUST
SUNDAY TO THURSDAY
AND BANK HOLIDAY MONDAYS
2.30 – 5.30
ENTRY MAIN GATE 50 YARDS ➞

After the siege most of the defences around Tiverton Castle were demolished, though a few towers and stretches of wall survive. The comfortable house that was built in their place is open to the public on various days through the year.

THE WALK

1. In Tiverton follow signs to the castle, the entrance to which stands at the junction of St Peter Street and Park Hill.

By noon on 18 October Fairfax had got his artillery into position both here and on the west bank of the Exe, so that his fire could attack both sides of the castle at once. The gunners opened fire immediately, but one of the first buildings to be hit was not the castle, but the nearby Church of St Peter. A chantry chapel, famously the finest in Devon, was reduced to rubble. Such damage obviously did not bother Fairfax's gunners too much for the church continued to take hits from cannon balls.

2. Visit the church to view the damage done by the Parliamentary gunners and the repairs that were made once the battle was over.

Despite the pounding they were receiving, the Royalists held firm. According to the conventions of the day a garrison was given two chances to negotiate a surrender. The first came when the attackers first arrived. At this point an agreement might be reached to surrender by a specified date unless help arrived. This would avoid the need for any actual fighting and was often welcomed by both sides. If an early date was agreed, it was usual for the garrison to be granted generous terms, perhaps allowing them to leave with their weapons and possessions so that they could rejoin their army elsewhere. If the attackers were faced by a long delay, however, they might insist that the garrison be taken prisoner. The details could be many and varied, and the talks could drag on for days. At Tiverton the garrison refused to negotiate at all, so a fighting siege was begun.

3. **Tiverton Castle is privately owned and is open to the public most days between Easter and October. Although part of the castle was demolished in the eighteenth century and replaced by a Georgian mansion enough remains to give a good idea of how it appeared in 1646. There is also an impressive collection of arms and armour, much of it dating from the Civil War period, on display.**

Having visited the castle, if it is open, return to the clear area in front of the main gates. It was here that a lucky Parliamentarian gunner scored a devastating hit during the afternoon of 20 October. In the words of Fairfax's report (written in the third person as was then the rule):

> And after many shot that we had made against them, a cannonier by one shot gallantly performed this businesse, for he broke the chaine of the draw-bridge with a bullet, which passeth over the entrance of the castle, which falling down the chaine being so broken, our souldiers fell on without any further order, they being loth to lose such an opportunitie and loving rather to fight than to look on when God gives them such occasion, which took good effect for they soone possessed themslelves of all.

Custom dictated that Fairfax should now offer the garrison a second chance to surrender. This time there were conventionally no talks or negotiations. The attackers could offer whatever terms they liked on a take it or leave it basis. If the garrison refused their lives were forfeit and they could be killed out of hand when the attackers broke in.

Fairfax continues:

Such is the General and his desire to spare the effusion of bloud as much as may be, that notwithstanding they (his soldiers) took it by storme, yet he himself gave command that quarter should be given to all those who were alive. Wee took in the castle Sir Gilbert Talbot who was the Governour of the place, 20 other Officers, 200 souldiers, four peece of Ordnance, good store of armes and ammuniton and abundance of treasure, which was divided amongst the souldiers.

The siege was over.

After the surrender Fairfax made Tiverton Castle his headquarters for the winter. The town was turned into an armed fortress as the Parliamentarians poured in the men, munitions and supplies that they were going to use in the coming campaign to clear Devon and Cornwall of the king's supporters.

14. BOVEY HEATH
1646

Distance:	4 miles.
Terrain:	Surfaced lanes only.
Public transport:	Stagecoach bus route 39 runs to Bovey Tracey from Exeter.
Parking:	Car parks and on-street parking in the village.
Refreshments:	Two pubs in Bovey Tracey, and one shop selling snacks and soft drinks.

Having taken Tiverton, the Parliamentarian commander, Sir Thomas Fairfax decided that his next move would be to capture Exeter. The city was then a key port and would make a useful supply base for the Roundheads for their planned invasion of Cornwall the following spring. It was also a hotbed of Royalist support that Fairfax could not afford to leave in his rear.

No sooner had Fairfax's men surrounded the city, however, than dreadful winter weather closed in. Rather than conduct a siege against Exeter's strong walls in deep snow and ice, Fairfax decided to starve the city into surrender. This allowed him to keep his men in winter quarters, with only those actively engaged on blockade duties braving the winter weather. Seeing this move the Royalist commander in the area, Sir Ralph Hopton likewise put his men into winter quarters. Unlike Fairfax, Hopton had no sources of supply from outside the area so he had to source all his army's food from within Devon and Cornwall. He did not want to alienate the locals by overburdening them, so he spread his forces out across the two counties.

A force of three Royalist cavalry regiments were put at Bovey Tracey under the command of Lord Wentworth. His main task was to keep his men trained and fit through the winter ready for action in the spring, but he was also expected to patrol actively toward Exeter to keep an eye on the Parliamentarians. On 8 January 1646 an exceptionally heavy fall

△ Cromwell and his troopers entered Bovey Tracey down this street as they rode in from Honiton. They fanned out to search the small town before moving out to face the main Royalist force.

▷ The old Manor House in East Street. It was from the corner window on the ground floor that a quick-thinking Cavalier threw a purse of coins to delay the Roundhead troopers, so giving himself and his comrades time to escape out through the back of the building.

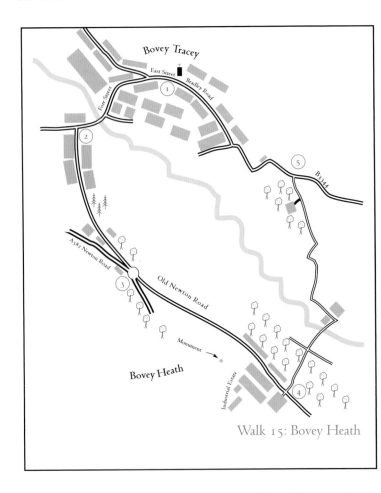

Walk 15: Bovey Heath

of snow came down on Devon. Wentworth called off his patrols over the snowy landscape and gave his men a couple of days off.

Oliver Cromwell, Fairfax's cavalry commander, viewed the snow very differently. He saw the hard, frozen ground as a great improvement on the slushy mud that had covered the roads in previous weeks.

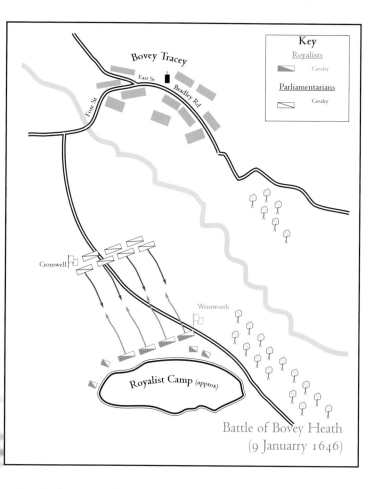

Battle of Bovey Heath
(9 Januarry 1646)

At last his horses could move quickly and easily. Cromwell decided to lead his cavalry on a reconnaissance in force towards Bovey Tracey and Wentworth's men. From his base at Crediton, Cromwell led his men cross country so that they came into Bovey Tracey from the north. It was just after lunchtime on 9 January when they arrived.

The Cromwell Arms takes its name from the Roundhead commander in the battle. Cromwell rode past here on his way to face the Cavaliers up on Bovey Heath outside the town.

The bridge over the river at the bottom of Fore Street. It was here that Cromwell led his cavalry over the river and headed towards the Royalist camp up on the heath.

The walk follows the Old Newton Road from Bovey Tracey up to Bovey Heath. On the day of the battle this was the main road, but it is now a quiet side road since most through traffic uses the new bypass to the west.

THE WALK

1. **In Bovey Tracey find the old parish church in Bradley Street. Leave the church and turn right to head west along Bradley Street and into East Street. On your left you will find the old Tudor Manor House, which served as an inn in 1646.**

Cromwell and his men managed to get right into Bovey Tracey without being seen. Arriving in East Street, Cromwell sent half a dozen troopers toward the Manor House to search it. Unknown to Cromwell, a group of senior Cavalier officers were enjoying a post-lunch game of cards in the front room. One Cavalier looked out the window to see what the noise was and was astonished to see the squad of advancing Roundheads. Reacting quickly, he scooped up the piles of coins on the gaming table and threw them toward the

Roundhead troopers, then took to his heels. While the Parliamentarians were scrabbling for the coins, the Royalist officers scrambled out the windows, mounted up and rode at top speed towards their camp on the other side of the river. One unfortunate major who was dozing off his rather alcoholic lunch was captured by the Roundheads as he slept.

Realising that the alarm had been given, Cromwell turned his force to the west and ordered an immediate attack on the Royalist camp.

2. Continue west along East Street, bearing left into Fore Street. Cross the River Bovey and then turn left into Newton Road. Follow this road for over half a mile to a roundabout where it meets the A382, a modern bypass road.

It was along this route that Cromwell led his Roundhead regiments at a brisk trot. He halted his men about where the roundabout now stands ready for the attack.

In front of him was a scene of frantic action. Wentworth had built a substantial camp for himself and his men. There were stout wooden huts for the men and rather flimsier stables for the horses. This temporary village was surrounded by rudimentary earthworks and a wooden fence that was intended to coral the horses as much as to provide a defence. The camp lay about 400 yards south-east of the roundabout.

Although Wentworth had been taken entirely by surprise, he reacted with commendable speed once he realised that Cromwell was on the scene. By the time the Roundheads were drawn up on the edge of the heath, Wentworth had about half his men in the saddle and ready to fight. Guessing that the enemy were not yet properly formed up, Cromwell drew his sword and led his cavalry forward in a spirited, headlong charge over the frozen ground.

The sign on a fence on the west side of Old Newton Road that identifies the stile over which to enter Bovey Heath to find the battle monument.

A view across Bovey Heath. At the time of the battle the heath was about ten times as large as it is today. The construction of the modern bypass and an extensive industrial estate has swallowed up large areas.

The battle monument on Bovey Heath. The boulder features an information board that tells the story of the battle.

3. At the roundabout take the Old Newton Road heading south-east, ignoring the modern A382 Newton Road which did not then exist. After about 500 yards you will find an industrial unit on your left. A stile on the right gives access to the Bovey Heath Nature Reserve. Climb over the stile and bear left across the heath. About 300 yards away you will see a stone boulder, which on closer inspection is a monument to the battle.

This is where the two forces of cavalry clashed. The Royalists had the advantage of the slight slope, but the Roundheads were better prepared and in tighter formation. The swirling, sweeping cavalry action ranged widely across the heath, then more extensive than it is today, for some time. Eventually, however, the Cavaliers broke and rode off to the south-west, leaving many wounded to be taken prisoner. Cromwell called his men back from the pursuit for by this time

This slope on the heath has been artificially steepened at some date in the past and is generally considered to be part of the earthworks that surrounded the Royalist camp.

It was almost dusk and he did not want to risk losing men to an ambush. He rounded up the large herd of cattle that the Royalists had been using to supply them with winter food.

4. Return to Old Newton Road and continue along it for about 350 yards, then turn left into a lane that crosses a railway line then passes through woodland before crossing the River Bovey. Follow this lane as it twists and turns over the water meadows until it reaches the B3344.

5. Turn left, then turn right into Bradley Road on the edge of the village and follow this road back to the church.

It was here in the centre of the village that Cromwell took stock of the situation before heading back toward Crediton. He had captured about 300 horses, plus a number of wounded Cavaliers. He had lost very few men. Leaving the dead to be buried by the locals, Cromwell rode off through the stone arch that now bears his name and left the area.

The battle served to establish the superiority of the Parliamentarian forces over those of Hopton and it affected morale among the two armies accordingly. Parliament now most definitely had the upper hand in the Civil War.

After visiting the heath, the walk returns to Bovey Tracey by way of this lane which can be both muddy and wet after rain.

15. DARTMOUTH
1646

The information board in the car park at Dartmouth Castle gives an excellent overview of the area.

Terrain:	Dartmouth castle is open to the public and there are no difficult surfaces to be encountered. The climb up to the Gallant's Bower is, however, extremely steep and poorly surfaced.
Public transport:	Railway station at Kingswear, connected to Dartmouth by a ferry while Stagecoach bus route 111 runs to Dartmouth from Totnes.
Parking:	A small car park at Dartmouth Castle.
Refreshments:	A café at the castle, plus several pubs serving meals and shops selling snacks and soft drinks in Dartmouth.

▷ The round tower of Dartmouth Castle was constructed in 1488 to mount cannon to guard the harbour entrance against French ships. This makes it probably the earliest fortification in England to be built specifically to hold gunpowder weapons. It was a key bastion during the Civil War siege.

▽ The view toward Dartmouth from the castle. Guns mounted here could dominate the harbour, then one of the most important in Devon.

On the far side of the estuary from Dartmouth Castle stands Kingswear Castle. During the Civil War this was a roofless ruin that played no role in the fighting. It has since been restored.

While his army blockaded the city of Exeter, Parliamentarian general Sir Thomas Fairfax set about capturing nearby towns and fortresses from the Royalists. Topsham, Powderham and Exmouth fell without trouble, but when he reached Dartmouth Fairfax found himself faced with a fight.

The prosperous port of Dartmouth had declared for Parliament at the outbreak of the Civil War, but had soon been overrun by the local Royalists. In 1645 as the war turned against the king, Hopton ordered the place to be fortified against a possible Parliamentarian attack by land or sea. The old castle, built more than 150 years earlier was updated and renovated. The castle had been of a revolutionary design in its day for it was the first fortified stronghold in England to be built specifically for the mounting of cannon. It was positioned on the seashore at the mouth of the Dart, its guns facing out to sea to guard the harbour against attack by French

In the nineteenth century Dartmouth Castle was upgraded to face a renewed threat from France. Most of the castle to be seen today dates from this rebuilding, as does this massive cannon.

pirates. Another gun platform was built across the river at Kingswear, though it was a ruin by 1646.

The fortress of Dartmouth was strong, but had the fatal weakness that it was designed to withstand assault from the sea, not from the land. To try to get over this the Royalists built an earthwork bastion on the slopes above the castle. Today it is known as Gallants Bower.

On 17 January 1646 Fairfax and a section of his army from the siege lines around Exeter arrived on the hills above Dartmouth, having marched by way of Totnes. Next day a small fleet of warships appeared off the mouth of the Dart, and sailed in to begin a bombardment of the castle. Fairfax began his land assault. The Royalists garrison did not have enough men to face both ways at

△ The entrance to the path leading to
Gallants Bower is marked by this
National Trust sign. The path is clear, but
arduous to tackle.

▷ The northern bastion of Gallants
Bower was constructed of earth in the
characteristic triangular shape of the time
and mounted a cannon. Today the timber
revetments have rotted, but the earthwork
remains.

The view out to sea from the Gallants Bower. Kingswear Castle is visible on the left of the picture.

the same time, and after a few hours of fighting the castle fell. The defences of the town were not so strong as those of the castle. The Royalists there held out for only a short time before surrendering.

The castle was guarded against an attack by land by an earth and timber fort on top of the hill immediately above the castle. The earthworks and some stone walls remain and are open free of charge to the public. A path up the hillside is signposted from the Dartmouth Castle car park, but walkers should be aware that the path is very steep, climbs over 300 feet in height and is poorly surfaced. It is no easy jaunt, but is worth it for those who can make the climb.

Next day Fairfax had his army ferried over the Dart to attack the fortified Royalist camp at Kingswear. After a token resistance the Royalists fled. There is today no sign of this fortification to be seen, the Redoubt Hotel having been built on the site of the action.

The eastern wall of Gallants Bower with the northern bastion in the distance. The parapet was topped by a timber wall and manned by musketeers

16. TORRINGTON
1646

Distance:	4½ miles.
Terrain:	Well maintained footpaths or pavements. The town is set on a hilltop and there is a steep climb down to the river and back again.
Public transport:	First Bus route 86 runs to Torrington from Plymouth.
Parking:	Several car parks in the town.
Refreshments:	Several pubs in the town, plus cafés and shops selling snacks and soft drinks.

After the battle at Bovey Tracey, both sides returned to winter quarters while the siege of Exeter ground on. Sir Thomas Fairfax and his Parliamentarian army cut the Royalist city off from supplies of all kinds. It was expected that starvation would reduce the city to surrender within a few weeks.

The Royalists were, by this stage of the war, outnumbered in terms of men, money and weaponry, but they were not yet ready to give up. Lord Ralph Hopton had been leading the king's men in the West Country since the start of the war. Although he had won many victories the lack of success elsewhere meant that he had been forced to send many men and supplies to help the king in other parts of the kingdom, only to see them lost. He was now reduced to a handful of veterans, but Cornwall and Devon were still staunchly loyal to the king so when Hopton issued a call for volunteers more men came flocking to his banner in Launceston. By the end of January he had about 7,000 men, more than half of them mounted.

There can be little doubt that the enthusiasm was, at least in part, due to the fact that Hopton had with him the dashing Prince Charles, eldest son and heir of King Charles I. The boy was only

▷ The town of Torrington still commemorates its battle. The signs for the town make this clear, and there is a museum in the town centre that is worth a visit.

▽ A banked hedge on the outskirts of Torrington where the battle began. These hedges are about 8 feet tall and made impressive field works that proved to be all the more effective as the heavy rains had forced the Parliamentarians to leave their cannon behind.

△ The junction of East Street and Well Street. The barricades around which the battle raged were positioned about where the red car is parked.

▷ An appropriately named pub stands in Well Street only yards behind the position of the barricades that were manned by Cavaliers during the battle.

fifteen years old and although he was in nominal command of the army he had been given strict orders by his father to do whatever Hopton advised.

This was a fairly large army by contemporary standards, but it was not well equipped and Hopton had little time in which to train it. He therefore opted for a strategy that would, he hoped, avoid any serious fighting until he had found the time to train the new recruits. He decided to march from Launceston to Barnstaple where he would pick up supplies of food and ammunition. He would then march east around the southern edge of Exmoor as if striking at the supply lines of the Parliamentarian army around Exeter. This, Hopton reasoned, would cause Fairfax to call off the siege and march back to protect his supplies. Hopton, however, would by then have doubled back to Barnstaple and Launceston to seek safety beyond the Tamar. With luck he would get away without any serious fighting, but would allow the citizens of Exeter a vital few days in which to restock their hungry city with food.

Hopton arrived in Torrington on 9 February. He was met by bad news. Fairfax had already learned of his move and was marching north toward Barnstaple, not north-east as Hopton had expected. It was now Hopton who faced being cut off. He decided to stay in the hilltop town of Torrington and fortify it against the oncoming Parliamentarians.

Torrington was surrounded by medieval walls and stood on top of a steep hill. These old works had been updated in December 1642 when a Parliamentarian army had previously been in the area, and now Hopton set to work improving them again. Every entrance to the town was barricaded with a temporary wall some 10 feet tall with a firestep to allow musketeers to shoot over it. Each of his infantry units was given a specific barricade to guard and houses nearby in which to sleep – they slept twenty to a house and forty to a barn. The church was commandeered for use as a supply depot and a prison for the Parliamentarian prisoners who had been captured during the advance. Hopton and Prince Charles took up residence in the Black Horse Inn in High Street.

Hopton had no artillery, which he considered a serious weakness, but he did have plenty of cavalry and dragoons – horsemen who dismounted to fight as infantry but had the mobility of cavalry. The bulk of these horsemen he put in a camp just north of the town, sending them out in rotation to patrol the roads around and to push toward Exeter to watch for the approach of Fairfax.

On 11 February it began to rain. By 14 February the roads were a quagmire, the men living under canvas permanently wet and the temporary defences drenched with water. If Hopton's men were suffering, Fairfax's men were faring even worse. They were on the march on the open road with no shelter and nowhere to dry out after the day's slog.

Fairfax had about 10,000 men with him, about 7,000 infantry, 2,000 cavalry and 1,000 dragoons. Like Hopton he had no artillery for the muddy roads had forced him to leave it all behind. His men were experienced veterans, all as well trained as soldiers could be, so that they not only outnumbered Hopton's men but also outskilled them as well. On 15 February Fairfax reached Chumleigh in the valley of the Taw.

At dawn next day the Parliamentarians mustered to march. The rain had stopped and the sun come out. One regiment of cavalry was sent riding fast to the north towards Barnstaple to block the route between that town and Torrington. The remainder marched toward Torrington. Fairfax was uncertain whether Hopton would attack, retreat or stay put so he advanced in battle order and with large parties of scouts riding out on all sides.

At about 2pm one group of Parliamentarian horse met a squad of Royalist horse where the road to Torrington had to cross a steep ravine and fast flowing stream at Whitsley Barton. The Royalists

◁ The western end of Well Street.
The walk goes to the right of the curved
building. It was along this road that Lord
Hopton rode after the collapse of the Well
Street barricade.

▽ The Black Horse Inn. Lord Hopton
had his headquarters here during the battle.
Oliver Cromwell was standing just outside
the front door when he was almost killed by
falling masonry.

fled, but the Roundheads had advanced only a mile or so when a fresh troop of Royalists appeared at Allin's Week. The two forces halted to watch each other warily.

At around 4pm the main Parliamentarian army came up, forcing the Royalists back again. Fairfax's men had not gone far when they saw thousands of Royalists in defensive positions. They lined the thick hedges and banks that cut up the fields just east of Torrington town.

The light was beginning to go by this point and Fairfax called a hurried council of war with his commanders. Most officers did not relish attacking unknown defences manned by unknown numbers of men at dusk. There were simply too many risks involved. They advised waiting until next morning when they could study what they were up against. Fairfax seemed about to

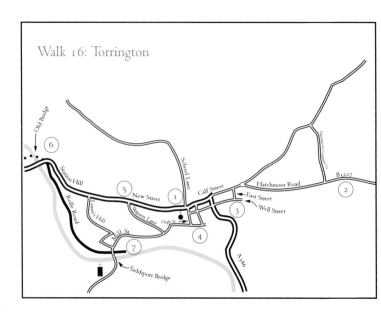

Walk 16: Torrington

gree when Oliver Cromwell came riding up. He had been scouting the forward positions studying the Royalists. He had seen that
most of the enemy were raw recruits and suspected that Hopton
would try to retreat under cover of darkness.

Cromwell forcibly advised instant attack. The others fell silent.
Fairfax thought for a moment and then gave the orders to attack.
It was about 6pm.

THE WALK

1. In Great Torrington find the parish church. Walk east
along Calf Street, the A386. Where the road turns sharp right
continue straight along what is still Calf Street, but is now the

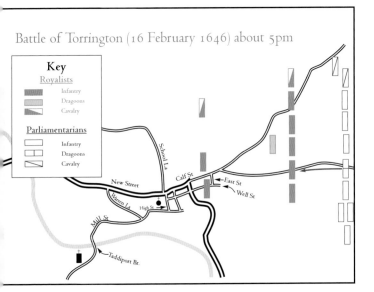

Battle of Torrington (16 February 1646) about 5pm

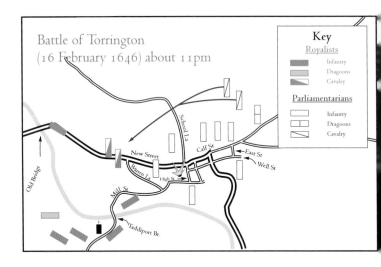

B3227. At a fork in the road bear right along Hatchmoor
Road, still the B3227. Follow this road past modern housing
until it meets Hatchmoor Common Road on the left and the
open countryside begins.

It was here that the Royalists had their front lines when the battle
began. The Parliamentarians were drawn up about 500 yards to the
east across the open fields. The opening move came when a group of
fifty Roundhead dragoons came up this lane, preparing to dismount
and fire their muskets into the flank of the Royalist infantry. But the
Cavaliers were too quick for them. One company of musketeers and
another of pikemen sprang over the hedge into the road. The musketeers fired a devastating volley at short range, then the pikemen
charged and the dragoons were tumbled into retreat.

This ruse having failed, Cromwell ordered a general attack in
conventional fashion. This was primarily an infantry battle as the
attacking Roundheads pushed the Royalists back from one hedge

to the next. Each hedge was stoutly defended and for an army composed mostly of new recruits the Cavaliers fought well. Only the greater numbers of the Parliamentarians helped them at this stage. One Roundhead officer recorded after the battle that he and his men had fought their way over thirteen hedges during this phase of the battle. 'Their foot made good with much resolution,' he wrote, 'and stood it out and fought very gallantly.'

2. Return along Hatchmoor Road to the fork, then return along Calf Street for about 100 yards to find East Street on the left. Turn left into East Street, then almost immediately right into Well Street.

In 1646 this street marked the edge of the built up area. The remnants of the medieval wall stood along the line of East Street. Both Calf Street and Well Street were blocked by barricades made of earth and timber. The retreating Royalists did well to fall back in good order, the men clambering over the barriers using ladders that were then pulled up behind them.

It was about 8pm by this point. The clear sky allowed the stars and an almost full moon to shine down, bathing the scene of battle in an eerie silvery-blue light.

The barricades were manned by a mix of musketeers and pikemen. The musketeers fired a volley as the attackers got to within 40 yards of the barricade, then leapt down to be replaced by the pikemen who used their 16 foot pikes to fend off the attackers, and their swords to despatch the few Roundheads who got to the top of barricade. The Roundhead officer recorded 'It was as desperate a service that was made since the march of the Army. Their men had the advantage of strong barricades and works and all.'

The fighting was now raging around barricades in adjacent streets, but the main focus of the Parliamentarian attack was at

Well Street. It was probably this that drew Hopton to Well Street. He had with him his second in command, Major Webb, Captain Harper, a servant named Thomas Cooke and a squadron of cavalry. Cooke carried Hopton's famous personal standard that had come to be notorious among the Parliamentarians. It was a square of heavy silk fringed with tassels and embroidered with the words 'I will strive to serve my King'.

Hopton and Webb were discussing the situation when a shout suddenly went up. A section of the barricade collapsed and Roundhead infantry stormed through. They quickly dispatched the Royalists on the barricade, then formed up into a compact mass of pikemen, with musketeers pushing through the broken defences to join them.

Hopton ordered his squadron of horse to attack, which they did but they were driven off. The Parliamentarian musketeers then fired a deadly volley. Webb's horse was killed instantly and Hopton's wounded in the head. Captain Harper was wounded and Cooke fell to the ground, Hopton's banner falling with him. Seeing the flag go down the Roundheads cheered and then charged.

Hopton, Harper and Webb fled back to the town centre.

3. Walk west along Well Street, following the route taken by Hopton. Cross straight over the A386 to continue along Well Street. At the junction with Potacre Street, jink right then left to go straight ahead into Fore Street, then bear left into High Street. The Black Horse Inn is on your right.

As Hopton pulled up in front of his headquarters his horse dropped dead, spilling him on to the cobbles. He scrambled to his feet and raced into the hotel's stables. There he grabbed the first horse he saw and rode out again. He emerged to find a scene of panic and confusion. Royalist soldiers were running pellmell to the west as the

△ The drop from Torrington down to the Torridge is high and steep, making town impossible to attack from this direction.

▷ The south transept of Torrington Church. The repair work after the dramatic explosion can be seen quite clearly as the newer stonework at the top is of a different colour from the medieval original below.

The church at Torrington. It was the stunning explosion of the Royalist gunpowder stores inside the church that ended the battle. The blast destroyed the spire and roof of the church and damaged every house in the town.

The old bridge at the foot of Station Hill is now no longer used by traffic, which uses a much wider modern bridge nearby. It was over this older bridge that most of the Royalists retreated after the battle.

sounds of firing and cheering came close from the east up Well Street. Leaving Webb to try to restore order, Hopton rode off to find the cavalry units that he had left camped outside the town.

Webb had no luck. The unexpectedly quick fall of the Well Street barricade had caused discipline to collapse among the Royalists. After a few minutes he gave up the job and rode off himself.

A few minutes later the Roundheads burst into High Street. They ransacked the Black Horse looking for Prince Charles, Hopton or any important papers – finding his paychest and with commendable restraint handing it over intact to Cromwell who arrived a short while later. Cromwell put a guard over the cash haul, then went back out into High Street to talk to Fairfax who had now arrived along with a squadron of lifeguards.

Cromwell had just started making his report to Fairfax when a devastating explosion tore the night apart. The concussion of the blast threw men to the ground and blew in doors and windows. A vast ball of orange flame was sent towering into the sky and almost every man in the town was struck temporarily deaf. The Royalist powder store in the church had exploded.

As Cromwell, Fairfax and the Roundheads tried to recover from the blast, large lumps of masonry began to fall down around them. A horse next to Cromwell was struck by a lump of molten lead from the church roof and killed instantly while all around men were being killed and injured. Nearly every house in the town was damaged in some way, with those closest to the blast losing their roofs and having several walls collapse.

4. At the north end of High Street take the alley that leads to the churchyard and inspect the church. The lower parts of the walls survived the blast, but the upper walls, roof and spire were all destroyed. Leave the church to enter New Street, the A386 and turn left. Continue west to the junction with Warren Lane on the left.

Hopton was at about this spot, then outside the town, when the church blew up. He was talking to Sir John Digby, the commander of his cavalry. Being further from the blast, the Cavaliers recovered quicker. Guessing the scenes of confusion that would be spread all over the town, Hopton ordered an immediate attack. Digby charged, but his men were able to penetrate only a short distance into the town before they came under a withering fire from the Roundhead Parliamentarians. He turned back and returned to Hopton.

By this time, about 11pm, Roundhead cavalry could be seen riding through the fields north of the town to cut off the Royalist

The high street of Taddiport, a village on the far side of the Torridge from Torrington. Those Royalists who fled directly south raced up this street to escape pursuit.

retreat. It was time to go. Hopton and Digby together organised a skilled rearguard action to protect the retreating infantry. Most infantry regiments had become hopelessly disorganised during the hectic escape from the town centre and were in no condition to hold off a pursuit by Roundhead cavalry.

Digby and his men made at least three charges as they fell back along New Street.

5. Be warned that the slope down to the river is very steep and long. You may prefer to visit the two bridges by car. If you choose to continue on foot, head west along the A386 New Street and pass the junction with the B3227, Limer's Hill on the left. Continue straight on as New Street becomes Station Hill and descend the steep slope towards the River Torridge. Just before the modern bridge carries the

After the battle the dead of both sides were buried together in a large pit in the churchyard. The mass grave was then covered by a cairn of cobbles, which can still be seen today.

A386 over the river, turn right into a pub car park, then left to find the old bridge.

Digby and Hopton made a last stand here, just on the east bank of the river to hold up the advancing Parliamentarians for as long as possible. The heavy rain of the previous week had made the Torridge an impassable torrent, so the defence was both necessary and effective. About 3am Digby finally took his men over the bridge and rode off after his comrades towards Cornwall. There was no pursuit.

6. From the old bridge return to the main road, turn left then turn right along Rolle Road, which is little more than a track at this point. Follow Rolle Road for about half a mile to reach the Taddiport Bridge over the Torridge.

This bridge was completely rebuilt in Victorian times and is now wider than the one that stood here on the day of battle. Large numbers of Royalist foot poured over the river here. They crossed largely unhindered as the Parliamentarian cavalry were busy engaging Digby's men on New Street and the Roundhead infantry were too dazed by the explosion to intervene. Once over the river the Royalists headed south-west toward their original base at Launceston.

At Launceston Hopton managed to rally about 5,000 men, but they were dispirited and lacked both pay and spare weapons. His priority now was to get the young Prince Charles to safety. The following weeks would be spent by Hopton and Fairfax in a complex game of move and countermove as they chased each other around Cornwall. Charles was eventually got away to Jersey on 2 March and just ten days later Hopton surrendered his exhausted army to Fairfax.

The Royalists were treated leniently by Fairfax. Most were sent home, though with strict instructions that if they were found in arms again they would suffer for it. Hopton himself was held prisoner for a short time, then allowed to go into exile. He joined Prince Charles and died in Brussels in 1652.

7. From the Taddiport Bridge walk north up the B3227 Limer's Hill, then turn sharp right into Mill Street. This steep climb takes you back up the hill into central Torrington emerging into High Street. Turn left and so return to the church where the walk began.

In the south-east corner of the churchyard is a mound covered by cobblestones. This marks the last resting place of the dead of both sides.

17. SALCOMBE
1646

Terrain:	Salcombe Castle is now a ruin that can be approached only at low tide and over slippery boulders and rocks.
Public transport:	First Bus route 92 runs to Salcombe from Plymouth.
Parking:	Parking available in the village as well as a car park at North Sands close to the castle ruins.
Refreshments:	Pubs and cafés in Salcombe and a shop selling snacks and soft drinks.

After the surrender of Lord Hopton's field army in March the Royalist cause was as good as finished in Devon. There were only a few isolated outposts and strongholds left loyal to the king. The garrisons of these places were suffering from low morale and a shortage of supplies so most surrendered as soon as they were approached by Parliamentarian forces. The men at Salcombe, however, decided to fight.

The castle of Salcombe had been built by Henry VIII and was still comparatively modern when the Civil War broke out. The heaviest and most modern siege guns would have been able to reduce its defences, but Salcombe was rather remote and the Parliamentarian commander Sir Thomas Fairfax was not inclined to go to all the effort of moving such cumbersome weapons to Salcombe. As a consequence he blockaded the place by land and sea, then waited for starvation to do its work.

That was going to take rather longer than Fairfax imagined. The Royalist commander, Sir Edmund Fortescue, had foreseen this eventuality and had spent the previous months buying as much dried and smoked food as he could lay his hands on and storing it inside the castle. Fortescue was under no illusions as to the eventual outcome of the siege, but he saw his duty as holding out as long as possible.

The view of Salcombe Castle from North Sands beach at low tide. When the tide comes in the rocks in the foreground are covered making the ruins an island.

While he kept Fairfax's troops tied down in Devon they could not march back to the Midlands where King Charles was holding out against overwhelming odds in the area around Oxford.

The Roundheads brought up some light guns and began a desultory bombardment of the castle, but Fortescue remained defiant. Finally, on 9 May 1646 a rider came galloping to Salcombe with startling news. King Charles I had been captured at Newark in Nottinghamshire. The news was passed on quickly to Fortescue who now realized that he could achieve nothing more by holding on. He surrendered.

The Civil War was over in Devon, though a few castles held out elsewhere for a few weeks more. There was to be a second, shorter, Civil War in 1648 but the Royalist uprisings and their suppression did not affect Devon. Peace came to Devon and never again were armies to march against each other across the county. But there was one last conflict to touch the county.

The castle ruins stand just off the large beach known as North Sands. It can be seen from the beach at any time, but can be reached only at low tide. There is no path as such, the visitor having to pick his way over boulders and rocks to reach the crumbling ruins.

◁ One of the pubs in Salcombe village is named after the Royalist commander during the siege.

A turret of Salcombe Castle that can be seen only if the ruins are approached at low tide. The crumbling nature of the ruins make it unwise actually to enter them.

18. SLAPTON SANDS
1944

Terrain: Slapton Sands is an extensive beach that runs for miles along
                    the coast around the village of Slapton. The going is good
                    and there are no difficult slopes.

Public transport: First Bus route 93 runs to Slapton from Plymouth.

Parking: A car park at Slapton Sands, where the walk starts and ends.

Refreshments: A pub close by the car park and, in the summer months, a
                    kiosk selling snacks.

The Second World War that broke out in September 1939 had a
profound effect on some parts of Devon, but left others untouched.
Exeter and Plymouth were both heavily bombed by the Luftwaffe,

The Sherman tank that serves as a memorial to the men who died at Slapton Sands in 1944.
The incident was kept secret for several years.

causing heavy civilian casualties. The naval base at Plymouth came in for particularly heavy bombing, and throughout the war it suffered the dismal sight of ships returning with wounded men on board – or of ships not returning at all.

By the spring of 1944 the worst of the bombing was over, though a few sneak raiders still came over from time to time. Instead the new focus was on the decline of Germany's military power as her armies lost ground in both Russia and the Mediterranean. It had for months been anticipated that Britain and her allies would seek to invade mainland France from Britain. Vast numbers of men and enormous stores of equipment were being brought into Britain in preparation for the attack that would later become known as D-Day.

A vital part of the preparations was to try out tactics for landing men, artillery and tanks from the sea on to the beaches of

The tank that forms the centre of the memorial at Slapton Sands was one of those lost on the night of battle. It was hauled back to the surface in 1984 and placed at the southern end of the long beach.

Wreaths of poppies lie beside the tablet that gives information on the battle as part of the monument.

Normandy where the invasion would take place. The military planners had been working on their preferred methods for months, but nobody was certain if they would work in practice. What was needed was a practical experiment, and that is where Slapton Sands came into the picture.

The planners wanted to try out their ideas in as realistic a fashion as possible. That meant finding a beach somewhere in Britain that matched the target in France as closely as possible. It needed to be the same size, made up of the same sort of sand and to shelve out to sea at the same gradient. Moreover the area immediately inland needed to mimic that of the invasion beach. Only then could the troops earmarked for the real invasion try out the tactics to see if they would work properly.

Teams of surveyors toured the country's coast looking for places that exactly matched the strict criteria they had been given, though none of them was told why they had to find beaches of such a precise configuration. Finally a surveyor came to Slapton and found that it was a perfect fit for one of the scenarios he had been given. Unknown to him the match was to the invasion beach code-named Utah. Not only was the beach identical to that in France but it was backed by a strip of marshy land fed by streams from inland that were of the same sogginess and extent as those behind Utah Beach.

The staff officers planning D-Day were delighted. They set in train the preparatory work for Exercise Tiger, a full-scale pretend invasion that would include not only the first wave of assault infantry and tanks, but also a second wave of support troops landing in numbers on to the established beachhead. The village of Slapton was taken over for military use and all civilians moved out. 'To be suddenly evacuated from their homes and means of liveli-hood at short notice was not a pleasant prospect,' wrote Admiral Leatham who was in charge of the operation, 'but they took it in good part, realising that their sacrifice was a necessary contribution to the success of the Second Front.'

The date set for the exercise was determined by the state of the moon and tides, which again had to be as close as possible to the projected invasion date of 5 June 1944 – though in the event the assault took place the following day. The exercise would begin with the first wave going ashore on 27 April and the second wave hitting the beach the next day. Field Marshal Bernard Montgomery, who would command the ground troops for the invasion came down to Slapton to watch, as did Admiral Ramsay who would be commanding the naval forces.

Exercise Tiger began badly. The warships carried out their preparatory bombardment well enough, but there was then a signals mix up which meant that two of the assault companies landed more than an hour before the rest. If it had been the real thing they would have been butchered by the German defences. When the main force did land they did so without the naval officer who was supposed to go forward with the lead units to spot for the naval guns. Consequently the naval guns fell silent for fear of hitting their own men, again a fatal flaw were it to be repeated during a real invasion.

Montgomery and Ramsay were deeply disappointed. Montgomery called the day 'a flop' and Ramsay rebuked his naval commander saying that there 'was much to criticise'. But things were about to get very much worse. Montgomery and Ramsay retired to eat a meal, then return to Slapton ready for phase two of the exercise.

That night naval ships put to sea from Plymouth and from Brixham. The little task force consisted of eight large landing ships carrying the American men, artillery and tanks of the second wave escorted by the corvette HMS *Azalea*. The naval side of the planned invasion was also testing its blueprint for assault by providing anti-aircraft ships and a protective screen of escorting warships.

Exactly what happened next is not altogether clear. HMS *Azalea* was damaged in a collision with another escort ship and forced to turn back. Nobody was unduly worried as there was still the naval escort and anti-aircraft ships. In any case there had been few Luftwaffe bombers over Devon recently and the German U-boats and E-boats had been inactive, apparently conserving their strength for when the real invasion began. The ships steamed for Slapton.

Unknown to the British and Americans, however, the Germans were active that night. A flotilla of E-boats was patrolling the western end of the English Channel in the hope of spotting some fishing boats or coastal cargo carriers to attack. These E-boats were

Slapton Sands stretch for miles along the Devon coast. It was their use as a training ground for D-Day that led to the disaster just off the coast.

fast, lightly-built motor boats armed with a pair of torpedoes and a mass of light guns, including anti-aircraft guns.

Somehow the German E-boats got past the outer screen of escorting warships without being seen. Since the *Azalea* was not present, there was no close escort to protect the troop ships. At 20 minutes past midnight, the E-boats went to work, firing their torpedoes into three landing craft, two of which sank. In all 638 American soldiers were killed that night and 89 wounded.

The event was a disaster for those planning D-Day, though with hindsight it taught the naval men valuable lessons that helped save thousands of lives when the real invasion took place. The news of the disaster had to be kept secret at the time. If the Germans had

found out that the Allies were practising landings on Slapton
Sands they may have been able to work out which French beach
most closely resembled it and so identified the landing grounds.
The next of kin of those killed were told that their sons had died
in an accident of unspecified type and the whole affair hushed up.

Even after the war the truth took many years to come out. In
1954 a small memorial was put up commemorating the sacrifice of
the people of Slapton in leaving their homes – most of which were
severely damaged during the training and had to be rebuilt. No
mention was made of the deaths during Exercise Tiger since they
were not publicly known about at that time.

It was not until 1984 that the present monument to the fallen
was erected overlooking the Slapton Sands which so many of those
men did not live to see.

The monument to the villagers is at Slapton itself, that to the
soldiers is further south at Torcross. The latter monument is difficult to miss since there are few Sherman tanks standing around in
Devon.

INDEX